NELLIE M^cCLUNG
NO SMALL LEGACY

BY CAROL L. HANCOCK

*Dedicated to the women of the United
Church of Canada past and present who,
in their many different ways, participate
in God's ministry.*

Northstone

Editing: James Taylor
Consulting art director: Robert MacDonald
Cover design: Lois Huey-Heck
Original cover art: Phil Clark

Photos courtesy of the Provincial Archives of B.C.

Northstone Publishing Inc. is an employee-owned company, committed to caring for the environment and all creation. Northstone Publishing recycles, reuses and composts, and encourages readers to do the same. Resources are printed on recycled paper and more environmentally friendly groundwood papers (newsprint), whenever possible. The trees used are replaced through donations to the Scoutrees for Canada Program sponsored by Scouts Canada. Ten percent of all profit is donated to charitable organizations.

Canadian Cataloguing in Publication Data

Hancock, Carol L. (Carol Lula), 1953-
  Nellie McClung

  Includes bibliographical references.
  Previous ed. has title: No small legacy.
  ISBN 1-55145-084-4

  1. McClung, Nellie L., 1873-1951. 2. Feminists--Canada--
Biography. I. Title. II. Title: No small legacy.
HQ1455.M3H35 1996   305.42'092   C95-911241-3

Published by
Northstone Publishing Inc.

Printed in Canada by
Quebecor Printing Inc.

CONTENTS

ACKNOWLEDGMENTS

The writing of this book has been an exciting experience of broadly-based cooperation within the community of the church. So many people from across the country have been involved in the production of *Nellie McClung: No Small Legacy*; and I wish that all of their signatures could appear on its cover beside my own. Knowing that isn't possible, I would at least like to gratefully acknowledge the friends and colleagues who, together with several communities of faith and learning, have helped bring this writing project to birth.

For her good-hearted patience in daily caring for our daughter Kate while I wrote, I owe much peace of mind to Dot Staples. The funds to help pay the costs of child-care were made available by the Anniversary Committee of the Women in Ministry Committee of the United Church.

For his encouragement to write my thesis on this topic, his wisdom in teaching and passion in learning, I thank Professor Ben Smillie of St. Andrew's College, Saskatoon.

Many women from across Canada read my initial manuscript and made comments and suggestions for improvement. Their wisdom and experience makes this a much better book than it might have been. I am equally indebted to Ralph Milton and Jim Taylor for their supportiveness and expertise while coordinating this project and editing the manuscript.

My husband Steve has given me the persistent companionship which enabled me to persevere on this work. He has been refreshingly helpful when words have eluded me and my sense of humor and perspective had all but disappeared!

The congregations of Grosvenor Park United Church in Saskatoon, and Zion United Church in Armstrong, B.C. have been, in their turn, actively and joyfully supportive of me and my work on this material, and for that I thank them.

I extend, finally, a very special expression of gratitude to Mark McClung, Florence Atkinson, Jane Brown-John and the rest of the McClung family for their patient willingness to share their personal memories of Nellie L. with the rest of Canada.

C.L.H.

FOREWORD

Nellie Mooney McClung is a timeless woman. In the '90s, Canada abounds with women who have spring in their step, as Nellie did, who hold to principles of conduct based on courtesy and justice, and who have a ready eye for the absurdities in the human condition. Nellie would have fit right in, say, at a meeting of the senior women of the Canadian Imperial Bank of Commerce, all of whom are senior indeed and smart as whips. The great Canadian suffragette would have been at home serving soup in a church basement shelter for the homeless, or a laundry workers' protest outside an Alberta hospital.

Someone asked the elderly Nellie McClung how she could have accomplished so much in the face of strong sentiments against women voting, let alone arguing a case before the Supreme Court or becoming prime minister. She replied sweetly, "We had a light hand with cakes and we weren't afraid of anything."

It has taken Canadian women almost 80 years to arrive at exactly the kind of person Nellie McClung was when she was a whirlwind force for change in this country. She was shaped by the spirited Prairie Methodist movement in the early decades of this century, which believed in what was called the social gospel, a doctrine which maintained that a truly religious person could not flinch from criticizing governments and other authorities who permitted people to suffer.

A system of beliefs routed in fairness for all could not exclude half the population from its protection, but most women of Nellie's era accepted discrimination against women as not only inevitable but also in their best interests. It required vision and doughty rectitude to see matters otherwise. Nellie McClung and her equally determined colleagues set in motion an astonishing revolution that shook the nation, but they did it with gracious good manners, intelligence, and iron wills. It was an unstoppable combination.

Today's women are of that mold. When the water rises, they can swim. Bright little girls entertain the hope of being space travelers or of building a bridge – and why not? Grandmothers learn to fly. Nellie McClung cleared the path. She established a style based on her observation that neither simpering nor whining get they job done. You simply muster your resources carefully, work collaboratively in dedicated groups, and stick to it. Every woman everywhere in this land is in her debt.

– June Callwood

A BRIEF OVERVIEW OF NELLIE MCCLUNG'S LIFE

1873   Nellie Letitia Mooney (McClung) is born in Grey County, Ontario on October 20th.

1880   Her family leaves Ontario and homesteads eight miles southwest of Portage la Prairie, Manitoba.

1889   Nellie, age 15, enters Normal School in Winnipeg.

1890   She begins teaching at Hazel School, near Somerset, Manitoba.

1892   Nellie begins teaching at Manitou, Manitoba and boards with the McClung family.

1896   Nellie and Wes McClung are married.

1897   First child, Jack, is born.

1911   The family moves to Winnipeg where the last child, Mark, is born.
        McClung's first book *Sowing Seeds in Danny* is published.

1914   McClung takes part in the "Women's Parliament" staged by the Political Equality League.
        In December, Edmonton becomes the family's home.

1921   As the first woman so appointed by the Canadian Council, McClung attends the Ecumenical Conference in London, England as a delegate from the Methodist Church.
        She is elected as a Liberal member of the Alberta Legislature.

1923   The McClungs move to Calgary.

1926   In the provincial election, McClung is defeated.

1935   Wes and Nellie move to their final home outside Victoria, B.C. The first volume of her autobiography, *Clearing the West*, is published.

1936   McClung is the first woman appointed to the CBC Board of Governors.

1938   She becomes a delegate to the League of Nations meeting in Geneva.

1945   Her second autobiographical volume, *The Stream Runs Fast*, is published.

1951   On September 1, Nellie L. McClung dies at her home at age 77. Wes dies in 1958.

PREFACE

Mark, Nellie McClung's youngest son, remembers the news broadcast which announced the election of Lois Wilson as Moderator of the United Church of Canada. Hearing the news he thought to himself: "Nellie McClung will be delighted in heaven tonight."

Listening to him say that, I felt my own delight – both at the sentiment and at the way in which it seemed to close the gap between Nellie McClung's generation and our own. Although each generation occupies its own place in history, sometimes the lines between past, present, and future blur, and we find collegiality and companionship in unexpected places.

Because of McClung's efforts, and the efforts of others who shared her goals and enthusiasm, Canadian women can now vote, be ordained as ministers, and enjoy more of the equality that is rightly theirs. Legally at least, no position, official or otherwise, is closed to women because of their sex.

I was introduced to Nellie Letitia McClung in my first year of university when her book *In Times Like These* was on my history class's reading list. (Lest you think that this was a sign of the university's understanding of the contribution of women to Canada, let me tell you that I think it had more to do with my professor being the general editor of the series which reprinted the work!) I feel that I first *met* her, however, when I did a research paper on the Persons Case, in which for the first time women in Canada were legally acknowledged as human beings. Perhaps I had developed the "eyes to see" by then. I became fascinated with this woman's work, and wrote a thesis on her for St. Andrew's College, Saskatoon.

Throughout these years I have had a variety of opportunities to speak with people about Nellie McClung. I decided recently that the next time

I have the chance at a public gathering, I am going to ask for a show of hands in response to my questions. Who remembers reading *Sowing Seeds in Danny* when they were children? Who heard McClung speak? Who knew members of her family? Who remembers his or her parents speaking of her? Who is related to her and her family? If my previous experiences are true to form, and the audience is not all children, there will be a surprising

Nellie McClung in mid-life.

amount of enthusiastic hand waving.

I have also discovered, however, that while McClung's name still evokes affection and even some actual memories of her, few know a great deal about her and her contribution. More has been written about Nellie L. McClung than about most Canadian women, but that still amounts to only a small body of literature. As a United Church woman myself, I was particularly interested in the way her Christian faith had shaped her work, but this aspect of her life has received very little attention.

It is my hope that this book will be read by a wide variety of people. Some of you will be quite familiar with McClung. Some of you will have little or no knowledge of her. This book does not bring forth hitherto undisclosed events, but it does try to present McClung's contribution in the context of her deep and committed faith, and to make her better known to the community of people that were always important to her – the community of the church. Nellie L. McClung's own involvement was first with the Methodist and then with United Churches, but she was not denominationally exclusive. Her understanding of "the church" embraced the church catholic – the whole body of Christ.

I have included fairly detailed chapter notes at the back of the book so that those who want to do further reading will be able to trace my sources. As a general rule, however, these notes do not need to be consulted unless such information is wanted.

Announcement

FALL AND WINTER SEASON, 1910-1911

NELLIE L. McCLUNG

Author of "Sowing Seeds in Danny,"
"The Second Chance."

Elocutionist, Entertainer and Reader

Mrs. McClung is prepared to arrange dates for
the coming season with Epworth Leagues, Ladies'
Aid Societies, Young People's Societies, Literary
——————— Societies, Clubs, etc., etc. ———————

TERMS AND OTHER PARTICULARS ON APPLICATION

Address:
MRS. NELLIE L. McCLUNG,
Manitou, Man.

Chapter 1

A Woman of Gifts and Means

When Nellie L. McClung was about 12 years old, she went on a trip to Brandon with her mother, Letitia Mooney.[1] They broke their trip with a noon meal at the Black Creek Stopping-House. Cold and weary from the morning's long sleigh-ride, it was good to rest in the large room where their hosts, the Corbetts, had hot meals ready. Mrs. Corbett was glad to have feminine company for a change and had her guests sit near the stove so she could have a visit.

The conversation ranged from weather conditions to selling wheat. Local people felt that the railways and grain companies had treated farmers badly. Mrs. Corbett said that it was about time that women had something to say about the way things were done. Mrs. Mooney disagreed. It wasn't a woman's place, she said. Surely, if men couldn't do something, there was no use in women trying. The men would have more time once they had a foothold in this new country.

Mrs. Corbett held her opinion. This was the time, she insisted, when everything was so new, for women to help get everything off on the right foot. She said that if she wasn't so busy feeding hungry men and making bread and pies in her spare time, she could think out a few things. Maybe young Nellie could do something when she grew up. "Maybe I will," responded Nellie eagerly. "I'd like to."

There was something prophetic about that encounter. Nellie McClung grew up to be one of Canada's leading voices in the call for women's rights. As a suffragist, temperance activist, politician, church-worker, writer, public-speaker, wife and mother, she had many opportunities to "do something." She did not set out to build a career in any one area but instead took opportunities as they presented themselves. Throughout her life, she repeatedly had to adapt to new geographical settings and life situations and her work was shaped by those events.

Beginnings

Born in 1873 in Grey County, Ontario, Nellie Letitia Mooney was the youngest of six children. Because she was raised by a strict Scottish Presbyterian mother and an Irish-Methodist father, religion was always a part of Nellie's life. She claimed that her own perspective was a mixture of both her parents' traditions. The family moved to Manitoba in 1880 to find better farmland and homesteaded near present-day Wawanesa.

Carefully taught that careers and homemaking could not mix, Nellie, as a young adult, thought she would prefer a career. She headed off to Winnipeg in 1889 for a five-month teacher-training program. The next year she taught all eight grades in a school at Hazel, three miles from Manitou. There she met her future mother-in-law, Annie E. McClung, the wife of the local minister, the Rev. I.A. McClung.

In spite of her qualms about marriage, Nellie happily married Wes McClung in 1896. She said that she knew even then that she would rather fight with Wes than agree with anyone else! She was soon pregnant, and by 1902 the first three of what would be five children had been born to the couple. It was in the midst of the chaos of children and home that she, with her mother-in-law's active encouragement and support, began to write – and she did find that time chaotic! As she noted in her diary: "with three small children and a house to run you can imagine the sort of frame of mind I'm in. In fact the frame is all that is left of my mind."

The McClungs moved to Winnipeg in 1911 when Wes decided to

Wawanesa, Manitoba.

change from his work as a pharmacist to a new career as an agent for the Manufacturers' Life Insurance Company. In 1914, once again, Wes's work instigated the family's move to Edmonton. There were two more transfers for Wes and Nellie – to Calgary in 1923 and, finally, to Victoria and their last home, Lantern Lane, in 1935 McClung died there in 1951.

If you had a chance to look through the many boxes of personal files which Wes gave to the British Columbia Archives after Nellie's death, you would soon see that she had a great fondness for notebooks and scrapbooks. From the time she was a teenager she liked to jot down bits of poetry or "quotable quotes." She often had no idea of how or when she would

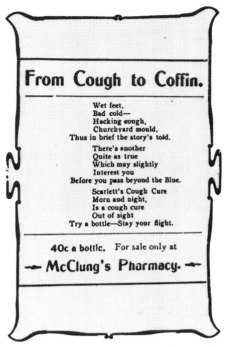

Nellie McClung sometimes wrote the advertising for the family business.

use them again, but for one reason or another they had caught her eye.

A quotation in one of her earliest journals really seems to fit her. In 1901 Nellie McClung had noted the following bit of wisdom: "A soft answer turneth away wrath," and the Scotch add, "and forbye it makes them madder than anything you can say."

That has both the impish humor, and a certain practicality, which often marked McClung's handiwork. A shrewd perceptiveness guided most of her actions. We can see clear signs of the judgment she exercised in choosing the ways she would go about her activism.

A WOMAN OF MANY TALENTS

Nellie L. McClung had a very well equipped "tool-box" of skills and abilities. She really was an eclectic – someone who picks and chooses from a variety of systems and sources. Her contribution has often been underestimated, I think, because people tend to focus on one particular ability and analyze it as if it were a whole career.

For example, if we looked at her just as a writer of novels and short stories, we could certainly find some fault with her literary style, and we might decide that she was not Canada's greatest author. The same would hold true if we examined her career as an elected politician, or put her practical theology under a microscope. McClung was a tremendously effective public speaker, but few would claim that she was a great orator.

Take any one feature and we can find weaknesses. What made Nellie McClung quite extraordinary, however, was the combination of talents she possessed and used.

I think that historians can easily miss the special mix of abilities which made her so effective. Nellie McClung put her passion into her convictions. There is no real evidence that she was out to make a name for herself in one endeavor or another. She did express early hopes of being a good writer, but she certainly didn't concentrate on that as a career to the point where she would have avoided other endeavors. Her writing happened in the midst of family, church, and political involvements.

Even if we consider her only as a writer, we can also see that she often adopted the style which would best serve her purposes, rather than work for art's sake. Look at the kind of writing she did. If we read only her narrative short pieces and novels, we might assume that they were the work of a traditional woman who had little new insight. Nothing could be more misleading!

Manitou Normal School

Nellie L. McClung had 16 books published. A number of them were collections of magazine and newspaper articles that had already appeared. Much of the material in her novels and collections was written as stories and many Canadians remember *Sowing Seeds in Danny* and *The Second Chance* as books they read as children. As with others of her generation, however, McClung used such stories to teach values as well as to entertain.

Even so, we might wonder why, when she had the ability to deliver sharp social satire, she did not produce more of that material and less of the ever-so-palatable stories. We know that she did have the ability. *In Times Like These* was published in 1915, the fourth of her books. Twelve more followed but none with the same sustained, focused, articulated feminist analysis of that one work.

NELLIE L. McCLUNG.

McClung's sharp wit appeared and reappeared throughout her public career, but she often used a softer voice. Some might say that she wasn't really aware of her own abilities, or that her critical hammer was rather hit-and-miss – that she didn't have enough control to be consistent. Even a brief examination of her contribution and its historical context, however, points to a different explanation.

THE SUGAR COATING

Nellie L. (as she liked to call herself) learned very early that some strategy of presentation was necessary to receive a hearing. Her warm, gently humorous, appreciative stories of pioneer Canadians disarmed and captivated a wide audience and opened doors for her. She soon learned to use those opportunities quite deliberately. When she was trying to gather audiences in Manitoba to hear her concerns about temperance and politics she agreed to present readings of her own work on one condition – that if she read for an hour, she could then address political questions for an hour. If that condition didn't work, then she hired the hall herself for the hour following the meeting and would invite the audience to remain as her guests while they talked politics!

Such sessions were highly effective. A contemporary wrote of her:

She has the gift of presenting political issues with a strong simplicity which captivates the better feelings and the more generous impulses of her hearers. Her stories and illustrations – where does she get them? – make their point with rapier-like incisiveness and sledge-hammer force. Her audience know her instinctively for what she is – a sincere, earnest, and fearless fighter." [2]

McClung clearly acknowledged that she'd had role models and mentors who influenced her and from whom she learned a variety of effective styles. Of her mother-in-law she once wrote: "She had a way with her – that gentle, soft-spoken woman; she had the strength of the meek – the terrible meek, who win by sweetness and gentle persuasion and the brushing away of all arguments as only the meek can."[3] On the other hand, she also knew that she couldn't just imitate someone else.

On first meeting the senior Mrs. McClung, young Nellie declared that she was the only woman Nellie would ever want as a mother-in-law. Nellie was just lucky that the McClungs had an eligible son! As much as she admired her mother-in-law, however, she knew that her own life would be very different from her mother-in-law's life as a minister's wife in a parsonage.

EARLY PRACTICE

Nellie Mooney McClung had been aware of different styles even in her own home. Her father's warmth and lively sense of humor contrasted with her mother's stern practicality. Such differences sometimes led young Nellie into trouble.

When she was little, her mother's two aunts paid annual visits to the Mooney's Ontario farm. Nellie described them as two thin old ladies dressed in black silk who always arrived with knitting needles and quick tongues ready. Her father, John Mooney, would retreat to the barn. He always had peas to flail when the aunts came, reflected the adult Nellie McClung later.

Rather isolated in their own home, this was the aunts' chance to talk and the opportunity was too precious to waste. They talked without pause and, usually, the two aunts talked at once. Young Nellie would sit nearby, drinking it all in – and receiving praise for being a nice, quiet child.

Then, as she wrote later, when she had gathered a good earful, she would head out to the barn and, with two bright straws for knitting needles, would re-enact the exchange for her father, carrying on until she was stiff with cold and he was tearful with laughter.

It was a delightful time for young Nellie and her father, but Mrs. Mooney disapproved of such "mocking" behavior. Nellie asked her father why her mother saw such harm in their fun. What made her mother different from them?

"She's Scotch," he said, "they're very serious people, a little bit stern, but the greatest people in the world for courage and backbone. The Irish are different, not so steadfast or reliable, but very pleasant. Irish people have had so much trouble, they've had to sing and dance, and laugh and fight to keep their hearts from breaking." [4]

Nellie replied: "I am glad you are Irish."

In writing once of the difference between two dogs their family had owned, she provided an interesting parable for her own family background.

O. I. SAY
TOWN HALL
To-Night
JULY 7th   8 p. m.

Will be the scene of the greatest rally to hear

NELLIE McCLUNG

ever experienced in Macleod

She is acknowledged Canadas greatest entertainer and oratoress and will be heard in her best form on the much discussed **Drink Question**

You can't afford to miss hearing
NELLIE McCLUNG
COME EARLY AND SECURE A SEAT

Old Watch had an unending sense of duty, she declared, and since he was never playful, no one but Mrs. Mooney liked him. Nap, in contrast, was a playful spaniel pup and very popular with the rest of the family. Mr. Mooney, McClung wrote later, said that it was a pity that the two dogs could not be combined:

> He said old Watch did not need to be so cross and grim and suspicious, and Nap might easily learn to be useful without losing one bit of his playful ways. People were the same. And then he went on and said that was one reason why Christ was sent to earth – to show people that a Christian might be, indeed must be, polite and pleasant, and full of fun and fond of music, and pretty colors and yet serious too and earnest. And he told me to think about this and try to combine the virtues of Watch and the friendliness of Nap in my own life.[5]

The blend of tenacity and wit with which she tackled difficult issues throughout her life suggests that she took her father's advice to heart.

MATCHING MEDIUM AND MESSAGE

The second volume of McClung's autobiography provides many insights into her awareness that the form in which an issue was presented really had an impact on its effectiveness. Temperance work was a case in point. In later years, reflecting on her work for prohibition, McClung wrote that she had realized that part of the struggle would be in finding a way to present the issue. "Prohibition is a hard sounding word, worthless as a rallying cry, hard as a locked door or going to bed without your supper." The liquor traffic offered tempting diversion from the grey monotony of life, she said, and the temperance women would have to make their own cause attractive if they were to attract support: "we must fight fire with fire."[6]

When McClung was a young teacher she had tried to teach temperance with the aid of charts and demonstrations about the dangers of alcohol but she was still frustrated by the limits to her message. She said years later that the Salvation Army had more luck with its color, warmth and music. She declared that their practical use of coffee, sandwiches, shelter and friendliness went a long way to countering the powers of evil!

Nellie McClung also learned that the way she presented her arguments and opinions had much to do with the reception they received. At one point she credited her friend Louise McKinney for an important lesson:

> I remember once I had prepared a reply to a group of some obstreperous women who were giving us trouble during the war, and I showed it to Louise, fully expecting that she would be pleased with it. I thought I had done a neat piece of

business. She read it through carefully and said:

"You've certainly demolished their arguments, but you have made them ridiculous and there is no need to do this. These women are sincere, though mistaken. It is never wise to kill your enemy, even if you can do it and get away with it. It's better to kill his enmity, and then you have acquired a friend." [7]

Humor was the tool that McClung often used to kill such enmity, and McClung's sense of humor, and her use of it, needs particular attention. I will look at that particular tool in the next chapter, but first let's look more generally at her skill with words.

A WONDERFUL WAY WITH WORDS

Nellie McClung wrote:

There are no idle words; words may be wise or foolish, worthy or worthless, honest or insincere, but they are never idle. They work overtime, and carry their own impact of good or evil, they can sear and wound, or heal and bind; they can darken the sun, or lighten the darkest night.

Words can build or destroy, inspire or defeat us. The gun is always loaded, and no one knows where the charge will strike. [8]

Believing this, it is not surprising that Nellie McClung knew how to catch and hold audiences. Whether in print or in person, she earned a reputation for effective communication. Wrote one commentator: "Mrs. McClung is a woman not only with a vision but with the rare gift of making

Monday evening, Nov. 9th, a

FOWL SUPPER

will be served in WASEY'S HALL, from 6 to 8 p. m., after which a Grand CONCERT will be given in the BANK HALL by local talent, assisted by Rev E. J. Hopper B.A., Mrs Nellie McClung, of Manitou, the authoress, who will recite and read from her book "Sowing Seeds in Danny" declared by reviewers the equal in laughter and sympathy to anything that Ian McLaren or Ralph Connor has written, and by Mr J. Dean I.S. M. Tenor of the London and Provincial Concerts, England, and more recently of Carman.

Thanksgiving.   *Full Moon.*   *Kings Birthday.*

Come and Celebrate.

Admission to Supper and Concert.

Adults 50¢.   *Children 35.*

Echo Press, Swan Lake.

others see through her eyes. To hear her is to never forget that for which she stands."[9] That last comment would have been received as a high compliment by McClung – it was exactly the reason for her speeches.

In her mind, if writers were to be true to their calling, they had a responsibility to be prophets. She knew that this wasn't a popular opinion. Playing on words, she said that many writers were dreadfully frightened of "propaganda," but there should be no shame in "propagating" an idea, if it was a good idea. To be a prophet, she declared, "may take courage and it may draw fire! But what of that? 'Woe unto you, when all men speak well of you!' Christ told his followers."[10]

There is something important here for us to notice. As much as she enjoyed working with words, McClung knew that the words were only as useful as the message that they conveyed. She said that she had learned that as a very young woman.

As a member of the Epworth League in Manitou, Manitoba, young Nellie was called to take her turn at leading a meeting. As was the custom, she was supposed to lead a discussion on the subject for the night. She carefully prepared a speech and she intended to present it without notes and be amusing. When the time came, however, she froze and on her topic "Spring" could only say that Spring would have to come without any help from her! The normally confident Nellie could not understand what had happened. When she realized that she had spent more time on the appearance of her speech than its content, she learned her lesson. That lesson was: "to have something to say which you think should be said and never mind how you say it, or what sort of figure you are making, say it!" McClung later declared: "Get it over to your audience as clearly as you can. If you can use beautiful words, crisp singing words... so much the better, but words are only the paper and string in which the thought is wrapped."[11]

Even fiction should make a contribution, McClung believed: "Literature may be light as a cobweb, but it must be fastened down to life at the four corners."[12] All writers, she believed, should have a vision of a better world before their eyes: "If you love your fellowman, and want to do them a service, with the gifts God has given you, hold fast to the faith, and the ethics of the Sermon on the Mount, which is the Common Denominator of all nations, and the only way of peace..." Writers, she maintained, "must hear the church-bells ringing, above the noise of the street. We promise not to be quitters, deserters, or neutrals, cynics or mere observers."[13]

With her conviction that a writer's art was only meant to serve a larger purpose – God's purpose – McClung cheerfully adapted material, even scripture, into a version which would most clearly communicate her message. As she put it, she would "smudge it over"[14] with her pen. A wonderful example of such "smudging" is her retelling of the parable of the Good Samaritan, an illustration she used repeatedly.

As she told this old story, there was once a man who was attacked by thieves and left, beaten and robbed, on the road from Jerusalem to Jericho. She said: "The priest and the Levite, when they encountered his broken body, fussed about the state of the times: 'Dear, dear, how very distressing, I don't know what the road is coming to.'" The Samaritan took the man to shelter and made provision for him, "... actually spending money on him."

Then McClung added her major variation.

In her retelling, the Samaritan traveled the same road again the next day and found another victim. On the third day he found two more and "... while he was caring for them, he began to do some revolutionary thinking – he hunted up some other good Samaritans, he even tried to interest the priest and the Levite, he hunted up his old shotgun, and they all went down the line, gunning for thieves. They determined to clean up the road!"[15]

The revised version of this story now led into her own message. Women, she said, were beginning to learn the same lesson as that good Samaritan: "For centuries they have been acting the Good Samaritan by their philanthropies, their private and public charities, their homes for the friendless, for orphan children, free Kindergartens, Day Nurseries; they have been picking up the robbed, wounded and beaten. Now they are wondering if they cannot do something to clean up the road. Investigation is taking the place of resignation."[16]

On another occasion, McClung used the same biblical parable but followed it with another more modern parable. The following excerpt comes from her chapter, "Women and the Church," in *In Times Like These*, and is a sample of some of her most effective writing:

> *In a certain asylum, the management have a unique test for sanity. When any of the inmates exhibit evidence of returning reason, they submit them to the following test. Out in the courtyard there are a number of water taps for filling troughs, and to each of the candidates for liberty a small pail is given, and they are told to drain out the troughs, the taps running full force. Some of the poor fellows bail away and bail away, but of course the trough remains full in spite of them. The wise ones turn off the taps.*
>
> *The women of the churches and many other organizations for many long weary years have been bailing out the troughs of human misery with their little pails... but the big taps of intemperance and ignorance and greed are running night and day. It is weary, discouraging, heart-breaking work.*
>
> *Let us have a chance at the taps![17]*

Those words still capture our attention. They still make their point effectively to modern audiences. In those few paragraphs she painted a graphic picture of the narrowness and futility of much charity work – without ridiculing the hard labor or the good intent devoted to it. The energy was misdirected, she showed, without offering insult. Church workers could receive her insight without feeling belittled by it.

Both in her writing and in her speaking, McClung's best work rang with conviction and passion. Her written word can still capture us with something of the power that her speeches once held over audiences. Of her performance on such occasions her son Mark has said: "My mother had a sense of the drama of making a public speech. She wasn't a passive speaker. She would walk up and down; she would gesture; she would point fingers; she would raise her hand; she would raise both arms... In a sense she was an evangelical preacher. She wanted to move people's hearts rather than their reason..."[18]

As a youngster, Nellie had discovered the writing of Charles Dickens and she said later that those books gave birth to a "deep and poignant longing":

As I read and thought and marvelled, a light shone around me. I knew in that radiance what a writer can be at his best, an interpreter, a revealer of secrets, a heavenly surgeon, a sculptor who can bring an angel out of a stone. And I wanted to write; to do for the people around me what Dickens had done for his people. I wanted to be a voice for the voiceless as he had been a defender of the weak, a flaming fire that would consume the dross that encrusts human souls, a spring of sweet water beating up through all this bitter world to refresh and nourish souls that were ready to faint... I remembered the lines from Milton about fame being the spur that makes people scorn delights and live laborious days. Yet it was not fame that I craved. It was something infinitely greater. I wanted to reveal humanity; to make people understand each other; to make the commonplace things divine, and when I sat on the flat stone on my way home from school, I thought of these things until my head swam and my eyes ran with tears.[19]

Her own first significant experience of public speaking came in 1907 when she was asked to give the address of welcome at a Women's Christian Temperance Union (W.C.T.U.) provincial conference. With her usual sense of humor she reflected later that the success of her speech probably owed a lot to the quality of the banquet which preceded it! Nevertheless she declared that whether or not anyone else would recall her words, the experience had made a lasting impression on her: "For the first time I knew I had the power of speech. I saw faces brighten, eyes glisten, and felt the atmosphere crackle with a new power. I saw what could be done with words, for I had the vision of a new world as I talked."[20]

POWER FOR GOOD OR EVIL

Nellie McClung learned about the power of speech from this early experience. But she learned an important lesson about the dark side of that same power at the time of the church union debates. The Act of Union which would join the Methodist, Presbyterian, and Congregational churches was being debated and a delegation had come before the Legislative Assembly in Alberta to present the case against Union. An elected Member of the Assembly at the time, McClung was deeply disturbed by the impact the speakers made. One in particular, a pastor of a missionary church and someone whom she had known and respected, caught the attention of his listeners.

I will never forget that man's appeal to us. It lacked all sense of balance, but its sincerity was shattering... He pleaded with us not to do this iniquitous thing. His eyes flashed like lightning in a dark night, and his face was white with rage. He ended with a declaration of undying defiance: "Give my roof to the flame, and my flesh to the eagles." Then he walked out with the proud bearing of a man of God on his way to the stake.

No, it was not melodramatic. It was something far worse. It was an exhibition of spiritual strabismus, the like of which I had never seen before. There was something terrible in it.

...that day I saw another side of this whole matter of religious tradition, and what a deadly thing it can be when divorced from the saving grace of common sense. No wonder Christ warned his followers to "try the spirits to see whether they be of God."[21]

McClung also discovered that there could be a dark side to her own quick-wittedness and quick tongue. Her son tells of the time she was in a heated argument during a meeting of the CBC Board of Governors – to which she had been appointed in 1936 – when she lost her temper with an opponent who happened to be a Jew. As Mark McClung described it, she said: "I was so annoyed with him I said... 'Mr. So-and-So, you're the sort of Jew that almost makes me an anti-Semite.'" Nellie told Mark: "You know, as soon as I had said it, I could have bitten my tongue. To say such a thing, to another human being – just intolerable." Mark said that she apologized to the board member with tears in her eyes and that they were reconciled on the spot.[22]

Such a lapse of judgment and discipline was extremely rare. Quick and fiery as she could be, McClung showed restraint and deliberation in many confrontations. She had a deeply ingrained sense of what it was to "fight fair" and that often curbed her passion. She was sure that the issues were bigger than her own personal feelings. With that perspective, and a great deal of discipline, she used the tools in her possession – wit, perceptiveness, personal appeal, communication skills, discipline, energy, persistence, and faith.

NOT BY WORDS ALONE

Although much of McClung's impact was made through her own writing and speeches, she was involved in a variety of other events from time to time which involved more action than reflection. Her involvement in the Persons Case, that landmark case which asked whether or not women were considered to be persons in the eyes of the law, and in an organized march in Edmonton for prohibition were two such instances. In that prohibition march, McClung was given much of the credit for an event which drew, from various estimates, between 10,000 and 12,000 participants.[23]

Throughout her public life, she demonstrated keen political sensitivity to the areas where she could make an impact, and particularly to the constituency of women for whom she was working. McClung described some of her own understanding of that empathetic sensitivity in her second autobiographical volume. The language is a bit flowery but it probably gives an accurate glimpse of McClung's own perspective on her work. She was quoting from a conversation with her brother Will. He had said that he could not see why she should appoint herself as an unofficial guardian and defender of women's rights. Nellie replied:

I know these people, Will... and they listen to me when I talk to them. I've had meetings in nearly every one of these little towns and in some of the school-houses, too. The women bring their babies to the meetings, Will, and that means they are determined to come. Women themselves are largely to blame for conditions. They are too much inclined to suffer in silence. They will not speak up on their own behalf and develop a martyr complex which is hard to break, but I can get closer to them than a stranger, for they know that I know what I'm talking about for I, too, have travelled the cold road and had my hair frozen to the bed

Nellie McClung at a meeting of the CBC Board of Governors.

clothes at night. I have warmed my bare feet in the place where a cow has been lying on a sharp October morning, and when I tell them these things I see their faces brighten and their eyes glisten, and they accept me. I have opened doors in their imaginations, I have made them see that life need not be all trials and tribulations.[24]

McClung's conviction that the necessary change could come about within the framework of Canadian society and structures would also have been less threatening than a more separatist approach. Even though she worked for the Liberal Party, she was not an ardent fan of party politics because none of the parties embodied all that she wanted. On the other hand, she never advocated the more radical action of forming a woman's party either: "'We could have... very easily... (organized one), and with some cause,' she later admitted, 'but while we would have had a glorious time doing it, we would have merely succeeded in dividing the progressive force of the country...'"[25] Instead, she encouraged women to exercise their vote collectively and, after study and reflection, to vote as a bloc when necessary.

Nellie McClung's humor, storytelling, political discernment, identification with the situations confronting women and even her eclecticism itself were all manifestations of her passionate commitment to her Christian faith and her feminism. Her son Mark has said that not only passion but compassion underlay everything she did:

(Her eyes)... were always filled with light. Whether it was the light of fun or of anger, there was always this light. She was stubborn and determined, but extremely compassionate, and whatever the situation, no matter how much she was against something, her compassion far outweighed everything else.[26]

As we are about to see, humor was often the tool which brought the light to dark days and bleak issues.

Nellie L. McClung, 1914.

CHAPTER 2
MATTERS OF LIFE AND LAUGHTER

Woman Suffrage is not a joke. It is not a humorous subject. I think it best to mention this at the beginning of my address because I have noticed from long years of church attendance that the mention of Woman Suffrage in the pulpit always brings a large round comfortable smile, just as on the stage when one of the actors indulges in real downright vulgar profanity it never fails to bring a laugh.[1]

That was the way that Nellie McClung once began an address to a ministerial association of the Methodist Church, and it is a helpful introduction to her use of humor. Some of her most humorous writing and speechmaking was formed around the topic of women's suffrage, but she was always careful to emphasize the seriousness of the issue itself.

Nellie McClung was not a humorist, not a professional funny person. She did have a deep love of laughter and a conviction that a healthy sense of humor went a long way to keeping a person healthy. She often credited her own sense of humor with restoring her perspective and balance in particular situations.

In addition to this basic sense, McClung also possessed wit. The two are different. McClung was able to translate her perceptions into words and images which allowed others to see the humor too. She had a flair for choosing, or creating, stories which caught her audiences' attention.

One person wrote of her: "Humor rippled through everything Nellie did. It was her ultimate weapon and the balm which softened her most outrageous antics. Even her wide-eyed brand of temperance was cooled by a whimsical understanding of human frailty, and her feminism was often sardonic."[2] Perhaps it was this use of humor which made her so surprisingly appealing to some who were the recipients of her challenges.

People who are now elderly, and who heard or saw Nellie McClung in action, seem to have generally retained quite a "soft" image of her. They recall that she "really was a lady" or that she was always so entertaining. Impressions of her lively speeches and her book *Sowing Seeds in Danny* are the most frequently shared memories.

McClung's work often had an artless air to it which was quite disarming. She wrote of herself that she had a "queer streak of cheerful imbecility"[3] before she finally, and painfully, learned a certain sophistication. Until then, she said, she had told critics that they would have to submit their case in writing if they wanted to hurt her feelings. Of this younger self McClung wrote:

> I would not take hints, I was always ready to believe no harm was intended. Naturally, I drew criticism. I broke new furrows, and attacked old prejudices. I was bound to step on someone's toes, and so did not resent criticism. I tried to follow Elbert Hubbard's wise slogan: "Get the thing done, and let them howl."[4]

That last line is quoted as often as any other that McClung wrote. Our generation seems to enjoy the confident assurance it showed, but it is not fair to her to make it seem as if that was her rationale for ignoring others' feelings or reactions. She was much too canny to proceed with no regard for consequences. Nonetheless, she was not willing to be paralyzed by fears of disapproval. Sometimes she just had to let the critics howl.

BAD EXPERIENCE

By the time she was in her 40s, however, this sturdy resilience to criticism had received telling blows. McClung said that she had lost something important, she was "never quite so sure of people after that."[5] One incident in particular, she declared, changed her perspective.

In the fall of 1915, she undertook a lecture tour in Ontario at the request of a group of women. (She did not identify the group, but Candace Savage, the author of a "scrapbook biography" about her, has said that it was the Ontario Equal Franchise Association.) McClung had been approached to add an extra lecture with any profits to be split evenly between herself and the group. The lecture was an outstanding success and the revenue far above expectations.

After McClung returned home, she received an unsigned letter stating that since the proceeds were so high she would receive a fee instead of her original percentage. She also received an anonymous letter threatening to make her name "stink in the nostrils of the Ontario people" if she refused to accept the change. McClung commented later that she still thought these letters expressed a minority opinion, and that she still believed she was dealing with honorable women. She wrote to the group saying that, "the success of the meeting was a poor reason for repudiating their own agreement." Then, she said, the fat was in the fire, and false statements were reported, first in the Ontario press, and then in newspapers across Canada.

Eventually, with help from various individuals and supporting newspapers, a different story was told and the money was paid in full. But McClung said that she lost something through it all. Some might say that she lost her naivete; others might say it was her absolute trust in human goodness. Nevertheless, some of that same confident tone remained in her work. Though it may have no longer been unconscious, it was still effective.

Nellie McClung at about the time of the final Persons Case decision, late 1920s.

Even in her early years, however, there is still room to debate whether or not McClung's humor always served to "cool" a heated debate. It could also be argued that sometimes it was the "fire to fight fire."

Although she often used humor to soften the pain of her jabs, she could also use her wit to make people as uncomfortable as possible. At times the humor stabbed with penetrating perception; at others it employed a more gentle touch. At times, anger permeated her humor; at other times, the humor holds only warmth and appreciation.

WIT WITHOUT RIDICULE

Nellie McClung's story telling was filled with perceptive wit, without ridicule. Such was the sense of humor with which she wrote about Pearlie Watson, the heroine of three of her novels. A delightful scene in *The Second Chance* is Nellie's "reproduction" of Pearl's minutes for a Ladies' Aid meeting, or as it has since been described, Pearl's "... well-intentioned record not only of the 'minutes' but also of the very seconds of that garrulous congregation."[6]

In the story, young Pearl was made the secretary of the meeting and, McClung said, being a fairly rapid writer, she was able to get down most of the proceedings.

The Ladies' Aid met at the home of Mrs. Ducker. There were seven present when it started, but more came. Mrs. Burrell doesn't know why they can't come in time. She told them so. Mrs. Bates said, Lands sakes, she had a hard enough time getting there at all. She left a big bag of stockings all in holes. Mrs. Forrest says it's been so hot the holes are the most comfortable part of the stockings, and if she was in Mrs. Bates's place she'd let the girls go barefoot. Mrs. Bates is going to let Mildred go, but she can't let Blanche – she's so lanky – she'd look all legs, like a sand-hill crane. Mrs. Burrell says, Let's open the meeting by singing, "How Firm a Foundation" but Mrs. Ducker says, Oh, don't take that, it's in sharps, take "Nearer, Still Nearer" – it's in flats, and Maudie can handle the flats better. Then they sang, and Mrs. Burrell and Mrs. Ducker prayed. Mrs. Ducker prayed longest, but Mrs. Burrell prayed loudest, and for most things. Mrs. Bates read the last report, and they said it was better than usual, she'd only left out one or two things. Then they collected the money. Nearly everyone paid, only Mrs. Burrell couldn't find hers, she was sure she had it in her glove when she came in and she couldn't see how it ever fell out. Mrs. Ducker will get it when she sweeps if it's in the house at all. Mrs. Williams had her ten cents in a tea-cup all ready, but when she went to get it it was gone, and she's afraid she gave that cup to one of the boarders by mistake. Mrs. Williams says that's the worst of keeping boarders, your home is never your own. Mrs. Forrest says if she only knew which one got it, she should charge it up to him. Mrs. Williams wouldn't ever think of doing that. Total receipts of evening, $2.20.[7]

There were two more pages of those "minutes." The tone is not derogatory but rather has the sense of intimacy which comes from identifying with the subject. McClung was not making fun of her characters, but she was certainly enjoying the situation!

We can see much the same style whenever McClung made gentle fun of herself. She often told stories about her appearance, for example, and cheerfully recounted comments which had been made to her, including the story of a little girl who said she wanted to watch her "throw her clothes on" since that was the way her mother said that McClung must have dressed!

In an autobiographical sketch,[8] McClung wrote of a photograph that she had taken once. This, she wrote, was a very carefully taken picture. She told the photographer that she "wanted a real good one." Affronted, the man gave her a stare which, McClung said, made every freckle stand out on her face and her hands go large and red. "Madam," he said sternly, "I think we can do you justice." McClung said: "I explained hurriedly that justice was not my plea – it was mercy!"

And one more example of Nellie L.'s portrayal of herself. She wrote of a time when a party of newspaper people came to Edmonton from the east. She and a number of her colleagues treated them royally. Later the oldest man in the delegation sent McClung a copy of his article about the trip. He had written: "When we were in Edmonton we met two women of note, Mrs. Murphy and Mrs. McClung, and both were a surprise to us... In the rotunda of the hotel we saw coming towards us a stout middle-aged person of kindly face and plain dress, and were surprised to know that was none other, etc. etc." "Stout! Middle-aged! Plain dress!," McClung repeated indignantly. "I am sorry he ever got past Sarnia! But that is not a proper way for me to talk, and I will take it all back. I have nothing against Sarnia."

Bear in mind that while she expresses frustration with those perceptions of her, she was the one delighting in recounting the episodes! There is ample evidence that this sense of humor was with her to the end. It is recorded that when McClung was dying there came a moment when she was very still and her husband Wes wondered if she had gone.

Her eyes opened again, however, and she said: "Oh, I'm still here! I'll never believe I'm dead till I see it in the paper." [10]

THE SHARP EDGE OF SATIRE

From this gentle humor Nellie McClung ranged to a use of moderately sharp satire which she employed for a wide range of situations. This is the style of the short story, "Banking in London," which has been hailed as one of her best. (That story is reprinted on page 129 of this book. The other piece reprinted on page 135, "How It Feels To Be A Defeated Candidate," combines something of both styles.) The sharper tone served McClung well in many of her speeches.

One example is the address which she made to the Insurance Underwriters' Convention in 1919. McClung used that opportunity to talk about an injustice which she had discovered. She said that she had been preparing for a ten-day lecture tour and decided to take out an accident insurance policy. Although she had often done this before, she said, this time she read the fine print after she had purchased her insurance and discovered that it provided excellent coverage, "... if the insured be a male." She said she wondered what the company had for her until she found an inscription, "... fenced off in black, as if someone were already dead..." which declared: "Females are insured against death only."

McClung told how she had sought out the man who had sold her the policy and asked him why women received lower protection for their money. She recounted that Mr. Brown "reminded" her that women, "much more highly sensitized than men," would be more easily hurt in an accident and/or would be much more likely to imagine injury where there was none. McClung quoted the conversation: "But, Mr. Brown," I said – "what about the clause relating to the loss of hand or foot? You would not be altogether dependent on what they (women) said about that would you? You could check them up – if they were pretending, could you not?" Mr. Brown only looked bored, and she said, "put on his glasses, in a way that indicated that he could not be bothered answering any more foolish questions."[11]

After repeating all the details in a highly entertaining anecdote, McClung made her point clear. She said that she was not surprised that insurance companies discriminated against women. It would be remarkable if they did not. The world in general discriminated, with the possible exception of those levying taxes and penalties for wrong-doing. In such cases "womanly weakness" was not counted as extenuating circumstance.

There are a number of things to note about this speech. As she often did, Nellie McClung was taking her complaints to their source. She criticized the insurance underwriters to their face – all indications are that they thought she was wonderful. The full script of the speech was recorded in *The Life Underwriters News* and the enthusiastic motion of thanks, with two seconders, was noted as carried "by a standing vote amid great applause." The fact that her own husband was one of the target group had not stopped her.

ANGER

Even such direct critiques as this, however, did not carry the anger evident in her writing and speeches about some other issues. Her opponents might well have felt that she showed little warmth when she was dissecting them or their actions.

The wit she used against Premier Rodmond Roblin in the years of struggle in Manitoba for suffrage was of this sort. Throughout the battle for women's suffrage Nellie McClung persistently argued that she was only asking for justice to be done. Suffrage was a right, not a privilege. She found it particularly aggravating, therefore, to hear Roblin's false and fawning expressions of concern for women. As usual, she had tried a direct approach. She met with the Premier and asked him for an opportunity to speak to him and his cabinet about political equality. As she recounts the meeting, Roblin told her that he honored and reverenced women and that he lifted his hat when he met a woman but he could not believe that women would want to mix in the hurly-burly of politics. Later, McClung commented tartly:

> *We went there asking for plain, common justice, an old-fashioned square deal, and in reply to that we got hat-lifting. I feel that when a man offers hat-lifting when we ask for justice we should tell him to keep his hat right on. I will go further and say that we should tell him not only to keep his hat on but to pull it right down over his face.*[12]

The opposition party, led by T.C. Norris, adopted woman's suffrage as a plank in their platform. McClung did not miss the opportunity of publicizing the government's sour comment that the opposition had adopted a plank of "freaks, frills, and fancies" which could only be supported by "long-haired men and short-haired women."[13]

One of McClung's frequent stories during this early period was the story of an old steer, Mike, which had belonged to her parents. Roblin

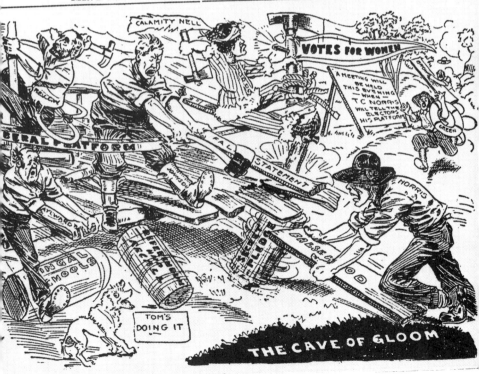

and company put her in mind of that cantankerous beast, she said. A minister of the government had been quoted as saying: "My mother is against it and my sister hates the very name of woman's suffrage, so you can't have it." McClung said that it reminded her of the time when she was little and it was her job to water the cattle. Mike the steer always demanded first attention, and was insatiable. One day, she said, she decided that she would try to give him all the water he could hold until finally he could only stand and shiver, she waited to see him move over to give the other cattle a chance. Said McClung:

Did he? No. He made a prodigious effort and rearing up placed his forefeet in the trough and then looked around as though to say, "see, I am the boss."

That is why my brain clicked when I heard that minister make that statement... I said, "where have I seen that face before? Mike, my old friend Mike, your bones have probably by this time gone to make fertilizer, but your soul still marches on." [14]

EMBARRASSING THE PREMIER

The most widely publicized example of Nellie McClung's wit came in connection with a presentation known as the "Women's Parliament," staged in a theater in Winnipeg in 1914.

In the early days of the suffrage struggle, McClung was part of a group called the Political Equality League. The League began with a membership of about 15 women. Their purpose was to gather first-hand information on the status of women in Manitoba, and in the rest of the Dominion, to train public speakers, arouse public sentiment, and to be ready to make their influence felt in the next election. McClung wrote: "We had all the courage of youth and inexperience with a fine underpinning of simplicity that bordered on ignorance, but anything we lacked in knowledge we made up in enthusiasm." [15]

As the group learned more about the position of women in the eyes of the law, they were increasingly appalled at the inequalities. McClung said that it was at this time that the incident around the insurance policy occurred; she now had the eyes to see the implications.

The group began to receive more invitations to send speakers to small towns. They began to look for ways to raise the necessary money. One of the members, Lillian Baynon Thomas, had heard about a skit put on by the University Women's Club in Vancouver. The idea was adapted to the local situation. The skit involved a reversal of roles for men and women. Women assumed the political places held by men and men became the voteless sex, dependent on the chivalry of women.

Although Nellie McClung played a central role in the staging of the skit, she was out of town during the few weeks of preparation and always gave all the organizing credit to the rest of the group. She later recorded the group's "plan of campaign." They would send a delegation of women to the Legislative Assembly then in session to ask for a vote. They were confident that Sir Rodmond Roblin would refuse. The delegation would go on Tuesday afternoon, January 27th, 1914; on Wednesday evening the women would put on their play at the Walker Theater.

The play would depict a session of parliament in which there would be a Government and an Opposition, bills would be introduced, heckling and inattention would flourish and then, as a climax, a delegation of men would be received; the men would eloquently plead their case for the right to vote. McClung was to lead the delegation to Roblin's government on the Tuesday and then "be" Roblin in the play on Wednesday.

McClung wrote later that her delegation was on pins and needles when Roblin rose to respond to their requests that Tuesday: "If he had only known it, he could have pricked our beautiful balloon, and taken the flavor out of every bit of humor." She was soon reassured: "He was at his foamy best, and full of the eloquence which Anatole France once described as 'that which glides but never penetrates.'" [16]

She sat in rapt attention, carefully absorbing every mannerism and cliche. All of it was material for her parody the next day. Since Winnipeg newspapers gave extensive coverage to Roblin's speech, it is still possible for us to compare his arguments with those that McClung gave back on the Wednesday. The Women's Parliament also received widespread coverage so we have a good window on the whole tableau.

Although McClung and her group counted on Roblin's rejection, the case she made to the Assembly for suffrage was just as reasoned and articulate as always. If, for some reason, the Women's Parliament had been undercut, there would have been no evidence that she had done an improper job at presenting the suffrage cause. Again, she was careful not to trivialize the central issue.

During the "mock parliament," when Nellie McClung presented her reversed edition of Roblin's arguments against suffrage, she echoed Roblin's patronizing compliments, his "fears for the home," his habitual self-congratulation and a fine summary of his well-known gestures and dramatic strategies. Her version also contained a number of sly but pointed hints of corruption in the Roblin government. These included references to the alleged padding of the voters' lists with false names and the improper use of funds. A newspaper account provides a glimpse of that evening:

The premier (Mrs. McClung) then rose and launched her reply to the deputation, almost every sentence of which was interrupted by gales of laughter from the audience which was quick to appreciate her mimicry.

"It gives me great pleasure to receive you here tonight. I want to compliment the deputation for their courtesy – and candor – and gentlemanly appearance... If all men were as intelligent as these representatives of the down-trodden sex seem to be, it might not do any harm to give them the vote. But all men are not as intelligent...

There is no use giving men votes. They wouldn't use them. They would let them spoil and go to waste...

Then again, some men would vote too much. Give them an inch and they'd steal a whole subdivision. They'd want to vote early and often. Even where elections are held only every four years, they say that once a man casts a vote he gets the habit and hangs around the polls all the rest of the time till the next election...

This is not a propitious time to ask for the vote. An unfortunate affair has happened in our own city in which men have been guilty of aiding a criminal. Records show that seven-eighths of the police court offenders are men. Of the church membership in the city, only one-third are men...

Politics unsettle men, and unsettled men lead to unsettled bills – which lead to broken furniture, broken vows – and divorce! [17]

Without an intimate knowledge of the time, it may be difficult for our generation to appreciate Nellie McClung's witty parody. It is rather like trying to understand political cartoons from a foreign country! Nevertheless she was immensely successful, and the group made enough money out of the presentations of their play to finance their campaign in the province. There was general agreement that a turning point had been reached in the suffrage quest. As one reporter wrote: "Never again will any politician in this province have the temerity to scorn women's power. If this election taught nothing else, it has made it certain that the women of Manitoba are not to be put aside with an idle word." [18]

IN THE CHURCH TOO

Nellie McClung's barbed wit was certainly in evidence during the struggle for suffrage in the church, too. I will have illustrations of this in the next chapter, on the work within the church to give women full voting rights and equal opportunities, but a newspaper clipping from the early '30s gives one example. The short article began by saying that McClung had the reputation for being able to "lay her enemies low in a verbal combat, but not without a touch of her Irish humor." [19] It then quoted a

story from the recent meeting of the third General Council of the United
Church in Winnipeg:

> *A discussion had arisen over the advisability of ordaining women for the*
> *ministry. Said one D.D. (Doctor of Divinity): "women would have to be very*
> *attractive before they could qualify."*
>
> *"It's a good thing looks were not a qualification for men in the past," Mrs.*
> *McClung retorted. "If you don't believe me look around you and these are all*
> *picked delegates. I'll grant you they are intelligent men, excellent men, but you*
> *would never mistake it for a beauty show."*

PROHIBITION

Nellie McClung's work for prohibition has not received much attention
in these pages. McClung's passionate speeches against alcohol advertising, sales, and consumption were not laced with the humor characteristic
of her other campaigns. Perhaps she did not want to give even the faintest
suggestion that this issue, all too easily written off as prudish and unim-
portant, had anything amusing about it.

Believing as she did that alcohol was directly responsible for the mis-
ery of many women and children, drinking was not a subject ever to treat
lightly. (A modern parallel might be found in feminists' willingness to
satirize certain oppressors and even some oppressive situations, but no
one would consider it appropriate to make jokes about child abuse or
battered women.) Nellie McClung did bring her quick-wittedness to this
battle. Although humor was not a primary tool, she substituted its constant companion, her picturesque way with words, in its place.

Winnipeg District W.C.T.U. Recital

In aid of the Building Fund
Tuesday, Dec. 3rd, 1912

READER .... MRS. NELLIE L. McCLUNG
VOCALIST .... MRS. GUS PINGLE
HARPIST .... MISS MABEL DOWNING
CHAIRMAN ...... DR. C. W. GORDON (*Ralph Connor*)

Programme

Introductory Remarks..............................By DR. C. W. GORDON

Reading from "The Black Creek Stopping House" by the Authoress
MRS. NELLIE L. McCLUNG

Song .... "The Valley of Laughter" ....*R. Sanderson*
MRS. GUS PINGLE

Reading ...... *Runaway Grandmother*
MRS. NELLIE L. McCLUNG

Harp Solo .... "Spinning Song" .... *Haffellmanf*
MISS MABEL DOWNING

Reading ...... *The Return Ticket*
MRS. NELLIE L. McCLUNG

Song.............. "My mother bids me bind my hair" .... *Haydn*
MRS. GUS PINGLE

Reading ...... *The way of the West.*
MRS. NELLIE L. McCLUNG

Harp Solo .... "Irish Airs" ....
MISS MABEL DOWNING

TEMPERANCE DOXOLOGY

Praise God from whom all blessings flow,
Praise Him who saves from deepest woe,
Praise Him who leads the Temperance host,
Praise Father, Son and Holy Ghost.

CHAPTER 3

WOMEN AND THE CHURCH

Nellie McClung wrote this poem as the opening words of the "Women and the Church" in her 1915 book *In Times Like These*. The poem summarizes the rest of the chapter.

Heart to Heart Talk with the Women of the Church by the Governing Bodies

Go, labor on, good sister Anne,
    Abundant may thy labors be;
To magnify thy brother man
    Is all the Lord requires of thee!

Go, raise the mortgage year by year,
    And joyously thy way pursue,
And when you get the title clear,
    We'll move a vote of thanks to you!

Go, labor on, the night draws nigh;
    Go, build us churches – as you can.
The times are hard, but chicken-pie
    Will do the trick. Oh, rustle, Anne!

Go, labor on, good sister Sue,
    To home and church your life devote;
But never, never ask to vote,
    Or we'll be very cross with you!

May no rebellion cloud your mind,
    But joyous let your race be run.
The conference is good and kind
    And knows God's will for every one!

McClung was frustrated with the confining roles given to women in the church, and was ready to stir things up to bring about change. Women were not permitted to sit on church boards or in church courts, and yet much of the financial requirements of the local churches were met by their work.

It is obvious, from her poem, that she rebelled against the patronizing approval with which women were "rewarded." In the chapter, she expanded on her theme:

> Women have certainly been allowed to labor in the church. There is no doubt of that... They may make strong and useful garments for the poor, they may teach in Sunday-school and attend prayer-meeting, they may finance the new parsonage, and augment the missionary funds by bazaars, birthday socials, autograph quilts and fowl suppers – where the masculine portion of the congregation are given a dollar meal for fifty cents, which they take gladly and generously declare they do not mind the expense for "it is all for a good cause." The women may lift mortgages, or build churches, or any other light work, but the real heavy work of the church, such as moving resolutions in the general conference or assemblies, must be done by strong, hardy men![1]

McClung also scorned the argument that the admission of women into all the departments of the church would have the tendency to drive men out. She declared that those who blamed the low attendance of men at church services on the "feminization of the church" were in fact admitting to a contempt for women and for women's involvements. Under this

Nellie McClung is in the center of the second row.

line of thought, if women were central, then the activity or organization had less value.

If people doubted this sort of contempt, she wrote, all they had to do was look around them for evidence. Small boys were taught to regard girls with scorn. Telling a boy that he looked like a girl or calling a boy a "sissy" was bitterly insulting. Being forced to sit with a girl in school was humiliating punishment.

Instead of challenging these opinions, she argued, mothers perpetuated them. It was up to the women, McClung thought, to call for the necessary changes, whether in their own families, the church, or society. She was also sure that there was something profound and involuntary about the silence of women. Why was it that women didn't put their own case forward?

At least some of the answer lay in lack of practice. Women had been carefully taught to play certain roles. In 1915 McClung wrote: "Women have until the last 50 years been the inarticulate sex, but although they have had little to say about themselves they have heard much. It is a very poor preacher or lecturer who has not a lengthy discourse on 'Women's True Place.'"[2]

Tied in with this enforced silence of women, McClung was sure, was a masculine domination over the teachings of the church.[3] The result was a loss, to the Protestant tradition at least, of the idea of the motherhood of God. The image of father God could not always be helpful, she declared: "There come times when human beings do not crave the calm, even-handed justice of a father nearly so much as the soft-hearted, loving touch of a mother, and to many a man or woman whose home life has not been happy 'like as a father pitieth his children' sounds like a very cheap and cruel sarcasm."[4]

SPEAKING OUT

Nellie McClung's own love of words encouraged her to break historic silences. She had a deep respect for the potential of clear communication. Perhaps her early experience of speaking to the W.C.T.U. made McClung understand the importance of women's right to speak in their churches.

For many people, the right to preach would quickly become the focus of the debate about women's rights within the church. Speech held power. As such, it posed a threat to those who wanted women kept in their traditional place. This focus on preaching was tied directly to the question of women's ordination.

McClung believed strongly that women's right to share the privilege of speaking the Word was a sign of citizenship in the church, and that denial of that right denied the equal worth of women. She had been actively pursuing equal rights for women in the church long before the question of ordination received widespread attention. Women in the Methodist Church were seeking the right to be voting members at all levels of the church courts. Opponents argued that if this were allowed, women would next seek to preach and that if they did, the standard of preaching would surely be lowered. McClung dryly commented: "There is a gentle compelling note of modesty about this that is not lost on us..." [5]

MAY THE ECLIPSE BECOME TEE-TOTAL

She thought that preaching, and ordination, were logical consequences of women's equal rights and that such rights were only in keeping with God's will:

> ...let me begin properly with a text in Genesis which says: "God created man in his own image... male and female he created them." That is to say, He created male man and female man. Further on in the story of the creation it says: "He gave them dominion, etc."
>
> It would seem from this, that men and women got away to a fair start. There was no inequality to begin with. God gave them dominion over everything: there were no favors, no special privileges. Whatever inequality has crept in since, has come without God's sanction. [6]

By the time the public and the media were ready to hear about the issue of women's rights in the church, Nellie McClung was a well known author and speaker, with access to the public ear. She published articles in a wide variety of newspapers and magazines. She made many public addresses in the years before and after the publication of *In Times Like These* in 1915, and her speeches repeatedly echoed the same themes. The following excerpt from one newspaper account is a fair example of many such speeches and, as such, it is worth quoting in some length.

Through the course of the evening's presentation she spoke about "woman's place," corrupt politics, "a mother's devotion," results of the war, prohibition, suffrage, the church, the church's reluctance to ordain women, prejudice in general, and the need for ideals. It is not surprising that listeners sometimes said that they found it hard to remember all that she had talked about! In her words about the ordination of women one sees her hallmark combination of cheerful, almost randomly recounted anecdotes seasoned with dashes of acid:

> The churches have preached resignation to us. "Men must work and women must weep." I don't believe in it. I don't believe in the weeping sphere. I believe that God intended both men and women to work so that neither would need to weep. Resignation is a cheap, indolent human virtue. During the great epidemics in the past, when multitudes perished like flies, the people folded their arms and said, "It is God's will." They were resigned when they should have been cleaning up.
>
> The Methodist conference decided that women must not preach. That is the church I belong to so I can say what I feel about them. We are all friends together. They said, at least one man said, that it would lower the standard of preaching...
>
> But I do not blame the brethren. An individual is never wholly to blame for anything. The philosophers have referred to women as "necessary evils." So many great writers have referred slightingly to women. One said that there were no good women, although some women came under the influence of good men.
>
> Still things are becoming better. The young men are growing up all right. And the old men are converted sometimes and if they don't change their minds, well, they die.[7]

In spite of that optimistic note, McClung must have been frustrated at how *slowly* such opponents died. She was an agitator for women's ordination for over 20 years before she would celebrate victory in 1936.

As the only woman delegate from Canada to the Methodist Ecumenical Conference in England in 1921, she made her opinions known when she was invited to respond to an address entitled "The Awakening of Women." Accounts of the reaction to her reveal delighted surprise at her directness. Her opening words took issue with the title of the address:

> The woman of 50 years ago who carded the wool, spun it, wove the cloth to clothe her family, made the clothes without any help from Mr. Butterick or the Ladies' Pictorial, brewed her own cordials, baked her own bread, washed, ironed, scrubbed, without any labor-saving devices, and besides this always had the meals on time, and incidentally raised a family, and a few chickens and vegetables in her spare time, may be excused if she did not take much interest in politics, or even know who was likely to be the next Prime Minister. But her lack of interest was not any proof that she was asleep – she was only busy![8]

After comments expressing her disagreement with the stance that the church usually took on issues affecting women, McClung spoke very specifically about ordination. She suggested that if the ministers who opposed the ordination of women had a real vision of the work of the ministry, they would welcome women to the pulpit. "They confess their inability to deal with the new spirit of unrest among women," she declared. "Does it never occur to them that though they have failed to reach the women, some one else might be more successful?" [9]

ORDINATION OF WOMEN

Church union rather overshadowed the issue of women's ordination for the next few years, but the creation of the new United Church did give some people hope of a fresh approach to the whole issue. Both the Presbyterian and Methodist churches had discussed the possibility, but to date had turned down any proposals for women's ordination. The Congregationalists, on the other hand, had always permitted the ordination of women, but none had been ordained in Canada. [10]

But soon there was a significant change over previous discussions. This time there was a candidate. As long as no woman had been ready for ordination, the church could avoid the issue by declaring that it was only theoretical. Why waste time on a mere possibility? Lydia Gruchy's application in 1925 ended that evasion.

It might be said that Lydia entered theology through something of a side door. Her brother, Arthur, had been studying theology at St. Andrew's College in Saskatoon but left to enlist when the First World War broke out. He had already declared his commitment to Foreign Mission Work. When he was killed overseas, his sisters Florence and Lydia expressed their intention to carry on his work. Both graduated from the University of Saskatchewan. Florence then trained as a nurse and went to India. Dr. Edmond Oliver, Principal of St. Andrew's, urged Lydia to enroll in the college and continue Arthur's ministry at home. Lydia had been working since graduation among new Canadians and felt that the children needed religious education. To Lydia, theological study meant a chance to serve those children's needs better.

LYDIA GRUCHY'S CANDIDACY

Lydia Gruchy graduated in 1923 at the head of her class and accepted an appointment to Verigin, Saskatchewan, as its lay minister. Her work there and at subsequent parishes at Wakaw and Kelvington continued the emphasis of her earlier work among new Canadians.

As an individual, there is little likelihood that Lydia would have given the abstract issue of women's ordination a great deal of attention. She said that throughout her theological training she had shrunk from all thought of pulpit work and had no desire for ordination. It was only the demands of parish work which created frustration for her. Although she had the same responsibilities as her male colleagues, the right to perform marriages and to celebrate the sacraments was withheld. She was widely quoted as saying to her parishioners: "I am a woman. You must receive the Bread and Wine on Sunday next from a stranger. I have to go and take his work. The church will not permit me to celebrate the Lord's Supper."

Lydia Gruchy wanted the inhibitions to a full expression of her ministry removed but did not really see all of this as symbolic for women in general. It was people like Nellie McClung who presented women's ordination as a question of justice. At the time, and even 50 years later, Lydia never felt that she had been discriminated against because of her sex.

When Nellie McClung asked her in a letter[11] whether her sex had been a handicap, Gruchy responded very personally about her ministry and said that in fact she felt she had experienced greater acceptance in Doukhobor homes than men would have had. She acknowledged that some people in Wakaw had expressed misgivings before she moved there, but that her relationship with them had been very happy.

In a 1975 questionnaire[12] Lydia Gruchy was asked: "What major obstacles, or special problems have you encountered prior to or following your ordination (family, parish or community, ecclesiastical)? Did other women and men encourage or discourage you?" She responded that she had met very little opposition and that since there was a shortage of ministers in Saskatchewan, she posed no threat. She said, "I accepted the fact that a man would be called ahead of me if one were available." In response to the second question, she answered, "I have always been cordially treated by fellow ministers, and given a full share of responsibility on committees."

It is evident that Gruchy's perceptions remained pretty constant. She did not think that her sex limited her effectiveness and she seldom broadened her perspective to the general issue of sex discrimination against women. In her letter to Nellie she did say, however, "I think it became apparent to others before it did to myself that the lack of ordination was a human barrier to the carrying out of a God-given task. I am convinced now that it is so, and that the same hindrance may impede the purpose of God in other lives than my own." Whether she intended to be a pioneer or not, however, her application for ordination became the focus for the church's attention.

When Lydia Gruchy, on Dr. Oliver's urging, applied to Kamsack Presbytery in 1925 as a candi-

Rev. Lydia Gruchy.

date for ordination, the presbytery referred the matter to the meeting of Saskatchewan Conference of October 1925. Conferences hold the power to ordain, but only to ordain those who meet the requirements set out by General Council. Uncertain about its powers in this instance, Saskatchewan Conference referred the matter to the General Council which would convene in Montreal in June 1926. Edmond Oliver was there to request permission to ordain Lydia Gruchy.

The request initiated a great deal of debate. Gradually it became evident that the question would not be answered by this meeting. It was decided that a committee should be formed to present the issue of women's ordination to Presbyteries as a "remit," and to collect Presbyteries' responses by the next meeting of General Council in 1928.

The Committee on Ordination of Women worked for a year to prepare a report which gave its recommendations to the church at large. A "Minority Report," included in the package, gave one member's specific advice against allowing women into ministry or even into the eldership of congregations. The Report itself suggested that the United Church set up a diaconate of women as a part of the order of ministry rather than give ordination to women.

ON THE OFFENSIVE

When the church considered the issue at its General Council meeting in 1928, Nellie McClung was a delegate and she served as the secretary of the sessional committee which reviewed the replies. She was upset by a number of factors.

For one thing, she had been incensed by the way the whole issue had been presented to presbyteries. In a letter to *The New Outlook* she charged: "Instead of being asked what they thought of the ordination of women, the Presbyteries were told very plainly that 'no action should be taken at the present time on the proposal.'" [13] Furthermore, McClung declared, the confusing and unexpected issue of diaconal ministry had been presented and "friends of ordination and opponents alike turned down the idea." A clear-cut, definite issue, she said, had been thrown into confusion.

When the responses arrived, McClung also disagreed with the way the replies were tabulated. Part of the controversy was triggered by the way the question had been put to the presbyteries. They had been asked to respond in one of three ways: "favorable," "opposed," or "approve principle but advise defer action." According to McClung, 33 presbyteries said "let's do it right away," and 43 said "we believe in the principle." She interpreted this as 76 in favor, leaving only 12 opposed.

Her arch-opponent, Dr. Ernest Thomas, interpreted the figures differently. He argued that there had been an overwhelmingly negative vote. He took the 43 "defer" responses to be negative and counted them in with the 12 "opposed" votes. He acknowledged 33 votes in favor but said that the 21 presbyteries who did not return the remit at all were "probably opposed." [14] His version received a great deal of attention.

McClung charged him with misrepresenting the findings of the committee. A prolonged and impassioned controversy between the two of them lasted for months after the rise of Council.

Because of sharp disagreement among the sessional committee's members during Council, the recommendations that they brought forward to the whole meeting were a compromise and not nearly as progressive as some, including McClung, had wished. The central declaration asserted that there was "no bar in religion or reason to the ordination of women to the ministry." No opposition was raised to the report, apparently because supporters felt that it at least opened the door to future decisions, while those in opposition felt that the liberal declaration need never be translated into action. A disappointed Nellie declared, "People can be too careful. I heard of a man who would not buy a calendar because he was afraid he would not live the year. I thought this was only a story until I sat in this committee."[15] Nevertheless, she supported the motion with its declaration and said that she trusted the church would soon put its words into action.

LIKE A MIGHTY TORTOISE

In the years following this 1928 Council, McClung spoke with deep weariness and disappointment about her church's slowness to act. Even in 1929, when she and many of her colleagues were rejoicing over the decision that women were at last officially recognized as persons in the eyes of the law, her celebration was overshadowed:

> We have still a grievance. Some of those who should have helped us, have been slow of heart and dull of mind.
> ... I record that with sadness of spirit. Of course the church did go on record. It said there was "no bar in religion or reason against the ordination of women" but it did not grant ordination to the one fully qualified and eminently successful woman, whose ordination had been asked for two years previously. But, as Mrs. John Scott, of Montreal, cheerfully remarked: "It is a forward step, when a great religious body admits the rightness of a course of action, even if it has not the courage to pursue it!"[16]

Elsewhere she wrote, "Even the church refused to acknowledge that we are normal human beings, with lives to live and souls to save, and an individual responsibility to God."[17]

It is important to note that even members of the Social Gospel Movement who eventually supported women's rights were not active advocates in the early years. Salem Bland, a major figure in that movement who, by 1915, was an active supporter of women's political enfranchisement, argued in 1902 against the admission of women to all courts of the church on grounds that women's voices weren't suitable, that their presence would "eventually undermine the courtesy that now characterized men's dealing with women", that the sexes should never be placed in situations that would make them competitors, and that such change would encourage the tendency to leave church work to women.[18]

In spite of her sense of frustration, Nellie McClung continued to agitate for the rights of ordination for women. A newspaper account of a debate in Calgary gives us a vivid glimpse of her witty public arguments.[19] Her opponent, Dr. W.A. Lewis, had told a story from his own experience which demonstrated, he said, the difficulties for women in ministry. On a certain occasion he had had to pull his horse and buggy out of a muddy slough without dirtying his suit before church. When McClung had the chance, she retorted that women would have been practical enough to wear old slickers and carry their good clothes in a bag!

Nellie McClung was not the only one who kept pressing for women's ordination in the years when no further action was being taken. Edmond Oliver continued his work and the Saskatchewan Conference continued to support Lydia Gruchy's request for ordination. In 1934 the annual meeting of the Conference resolved to notify the General Council that it intended to ordain Lydia at its next meeting in 1935 "unless at its meeting in September 1934 objection thereto is made by General Council."

Once again General Council decided that it had to hear the will of the Presbyteries before it could make its decision. After much debate and re-wording of amendments to motions, it was decided that Presbyteries would be asked to answer, with an unqualified "yes or "no," whether or not they approved the ordination of women. This also meant that no further action could be taken until the 1936 Council received the responses.

The United Church publication, *The New Outlook*, again carried letters and articles reflecting the variety of opinions. By this time most of the arguments were fairly familiar! Presbyteries took the votes and returned the results and on September 24, 1936 the report of the remit was presented. Of those responding from the 114 Presbyteries, 79 were for the ordination of women and 26 were against. With these results, a new policy was mandatory and the General Council ordered the changing of its *Manual* to reflect the new inclusion of women.

FIRST WOMAN ORDAINED

On November 4, 1936, Lydia Gruchy was ordained to the order of ministry at St. Andrew's United Church in Moose Jaw. Sadly, Edmond Oliver had died before he witnessed the event, but 1,000 others were there to participate in the service of worship.

In Victoria, where she was by this time living, Nellie McClung wrote an article entitled "The Long Road to Freedom." In it she expressed her reflections on the long awaited action.

It is a long time since Erasmus, in a burst of enthusiasm, said he would wish "that even women might read the Gospels!" but it has taken the full 500 years to convince the "brethren" and fathers of the church that women have the same ability to understand the scriptures as men, and the end is not yet. The road to freedom is a long and winding road, with confusing crossroads and detours, but no short-cuts...

The United Church of Canada took ten years to make up its mind whether or not it could allow a woman to be ordained to its ministry. Every two years the matter came before General Council; every two years there were speeches made, and committees appointed to look into the matter, and "ascertain the mind of the presbyteries," but finally in September of last year, the last hurdle was taken, and the matter was decided in the affirmative "by an overwhelming vote"...

So the United Church of Canada has at last endorsed what Saint Paul said more than 1800 years ago, that there is no "male or female, bound or free," but all are one in the service of God.[20]

ONE MORE TIME

Although McClung's part of the story really ended here, we need to add a postscript to the ordination drama. When Margaret Butler, a married woman with a child, applied for ordination in 1946, fresh debates opened.[21] Some thought that ordination had only been meant for single women, and there were prolonged discussions in the various courts of the church before Butler was ordained in 1947.

Because of the controversy, the "Commission on the Ministries for Women Including Ordination" was created. When it produced its recommendations it suggested that while ordination would remain open to women, pregnant women ministers should take a leave of absence or resign until "capable of fulfilling their responsibilities" once again. The recurrent concern was that women could not fulfill all their responsibilities as wife, mother, and minister simultaneously. Both the church and the family would be "robbed."

Parallels were not made to married male clergy with children.

In 1962, the Commission on Ordination brought more recommendations to General Council. Although the various suggestions involved limitations to women's eligibility for ordination, only one recommendation was officially adopted. It declared that ordination would be open only to those women who were unmarried or widows or who were "at that time in life when they are no longer required in the home as mothers" and if a suitable ministry could be arranged which did not interfere "with the stability of the marriage and their positions as wives" and that they were "therefore able to fulfill the vows of ordination." Even though the motion was adopted, there was fierce opposition and 62 men and women insisted on having their negative votes recorded.

This policy of restriction was very short-lived. The 1964 Council voted to remove the restriction and ordination has since remained open to all women.

CHAPTER 4

SPEAKING OF WOMEN

Nellie McClung once wrote a story about a woman who grew up in the shade of prettier sisters. This woman, Hilda, considered herself homely and was sure that she would never have a chance to marry. It therefore seemed quite natural and appropriate that she should devote her considerable energies and abilities to the teaching of children. She even specialized in serving geographically remote areas.

Now, to the surprise of her sisters, Hilda grew steadily happier in her work and even began to receive professional attention from her peers for her contribution. McClung wrote that she had known Hilda when she was young and then met her again when Hilda was called home because of sickness in the family. McClung thought that Hilda's work had really transformed her and that now her own special attractiveness had become evident. Always hopeful for happy marriages, McClung said that she told Hilda that she would be "snapped up yet" but Hilda replied very clearly that she was not looking for that. Hilda's contentment certainly impressed Nellie, who wrote, "I looked after her in admiration as she went quickly down the street, and I was more than ever convinced that the Lord knows what He is doing when He leaves some of the best women in the world unattached."[1]

That story may not strike our ears as very strange until we compare it to another that McClung wrote. She was always quick to give women credit and praise for the work they did for their homes and families. She knew that such work was often underestimated and overlooked and sometimes she waxed rather poetic in her attempts to right that wrong.

One of McClung's short stories, "Wise Women Know Their Own Value"[2] detailed a day in the life of a busy town homemaker. This homemaker, Mary, was the first one up in the morning and it was she who made sure that her husband and children, well fed, were off to their appointed places on time.

On the day that McClung described, Mary had a steady run of routine and unexpected chores to do for her home and family – from lunch guests her husband decided to bring home, to requests for laundry and mending. Late in the afternoon an enumerator called, asking for the residents' names and occupations. When it came to her own name, though, the enumerator drew a line through the space for occupation. He said that he usually left it blank because some women didn't like to be called "housekeeper" or "married woman." The story ends with Mary's reflection on this lack of a name. "'There may be no word for it, but I know,' she said, for Mary Wilson was one of the wise women of the world who know the value of their work. She knew she was the string on which her whole family was threaded: a cord of silk, smooth, strong, and enduring."

We might have a few thoughts about some of the demands from her family that Mary accepted so calmly, but McClung's point was that this wife and mother drew great dignity and satisfaction from knowing how important her own work was. She was "the string on which her whole family was threaded."

This story and its message would have been much more familiar to McClung's listeners than the story celebrating Hilda's single life. It must have surprised some of her contemporaries that Nellie McClung would value single life and other work for women as much as she did homemaking.

We can understand her position a little more clearly when we see what she wrote in an article called "Success" in 1916. She was responding to an anti-suffrage claim that women were forgetting their proper place, namely, to make a home for men and raise their children. McClung wrote:

> I believe that the woman who stands behind the counter, or over the washtub, or sits on the throne, who lives up to the light that she has and does the best she can, thinking kindly of every human being, recognizing her duty to others, and ready to help along, even at the expense of her own comfort, is a successful woman, whether she is the mother of ten children or none at all. [3]

That comment neatly expressed the understanding which lay behind the stories. "Success" did not come in only one form.

ROLES OF MEN AND WOMEN

These stories are a good place to begin to understand Nellie McClung's view of the world and the roles of women and men – when we look at her as a feminist. That word "feminism" is likely to raise a variety of feelings. Some of us use that term with familiarity and comfort, some of us feel uneasy about the word's implications.

For our purposes, let's say, generally, that feminism is the perspective which asserts the rights of women, critiques ways in which those rights have been withheld or limited, and works to realize such rights fully. It doesn't take much of a survey of McClung's life to realize that she was a feminist, but there is still debate about what kind of feminist she was. First, let's look at what Nellie McClung thought about women and their role in life.

Perhaps one of the best places to look is in an article that she wrote for *Maclean's* magazine in 1916; she called it "Speaking of Women." McClung was invited to write this article in response to an earlier one by the Canadian humorist Stephen Leacock. A lot of people are surprised to discover how strong an anti-feminist Leacock was. Afraid that the right to vote would encourage female independence and discourage marriage, he thought that having the right to vote would inevitably create career-minded women and that would take them away from their proper occupations as mothers.

A gathering to meet famous British Suffragette Emmeline Pankhurst.
Immediately behind young Mark McClung and from left to right are
Nellie McClung, Pankhurst and Emily Murphy.

Leacock had put forth his view in an article called "The Woman Question." Then McClung had her chance to respond. Interestingly, McClung did not directly attack Leacock's opinions, she simply laid out her own. She began her article by giving her own brand of lesson in prehistoric economics: "The Cave Dweller, long ago, realizing that the food supply was limited and hard to obtain, was disposed to look upon every other man as a possible rival, and considered it good policy to kill at sight in order that the crowd around the Neolithic lunch counter might be lessened." Even though there had been some development since then in the logic of cooperation, she argued, the old instincts died hard and there was still the "... ghost of that old fear that there may not be enough of some things to go around if too many people have the same chance of obtaining a share." It was this fear, she claimed, which lay at the root of much of the opposition to all reforms, including reform for women.

ECONOMIC CONNECTIONS

Here and elsewhere McClung made a connection between the social and economic dimensions of sexism. (Sexism – the giving or withholding of power and rights to people based on their sex alone.) Women, she said, were welcome to labor forever, as long as they expected no wage. As long as they were overburdened and dependent, they were occupying their proper place: "No person objects to the homesteader's wife having to get out wood, or break up scrub land, or drive oxen, so long as she is not doing these things for herself and has no legal claim on the result of her labor. Working for someone else is very sweet and womanly, and most commendable."

The same men who claimed that they couldn't bear the thought of women exposed to the hardships of the outside world, she pointed out, gave no thought to the cleaning women who tended their offices and then traveled home in the middle of the night when the lack of public transportation made them vulnerable in numerous ways. With stinging perception McClung declared, "The tenderhearted ones can bear this with equanimity. It is the thought of women getting into comfortable and well-paid positions which wrings their manly hearts!"

Nellie McClung made it clear that she had no patience for patronizing and obviously insincere concerns for women's "frail abilities." In the *Maclean's* article, she argued that the refusal to "overtax" women by giving them the vote was a "neat blending of kindness and cruelty." To underline her point about this sneaky masking of cruelty by an air of concern, she plunged into the telling of a story which seemed at first to be totally irrelevant. As with many of her anecdotes, however, there is a little sting in the tale!

> *Little Harry had a birthday party one day, and as part of the entertainment he proudly exhibited a fine family of young puppies, who occupied a corner of the barn. One of his little guests seemed to be greatly attracted by the smallest puppy. He carried it about in his arms and appeared to lavish great affection on it! At last, he took it into the house, and interviewed Harry's mother. "Oh, Mrs. Brown," he said, "this little puppy is smaller than any of the others – and Harry says it will never grow to be a fine big dog – and maybe it is sick – and it is a dear sweet pet – and please may we drown it?"*

Such "thoughtfulness" was parallel to all who offered deceitful sympathy to women, she thought!

MORE THAN MOTHERING

In the same article, McClung dealt with the perpetual issue, raised once again by Leacock, that women had to be the mothers of the race and therefore could be nothing else. She perceived that the argument neatly confined women. If they did not have children then they were undermining the future of the whole race – Leacock bleated hysterically about "race suicide." On the other hand, if they *did* have children then those children must occupy all their time.

McClung argued that even women who bore children and cared for them could not limit their whole lives to children's nurture: "... from observation and experience, I wish to state positively that children do grow up... and when they have gone from their mother, she still has her life to live." Following immediately upon that thought, she continued, "The strong, active, virile woman of 50, with 20 good years ahead of her, with a wealth of experience and wisdom, with a heart mellowed by time and filled with that large charity which only comes by knowledge – is a force to be reckoned with in the uplift of the world."

It seems quite clear that McClung offered these thoughts to answer even the most conservative of opponents, after all, she was responding to Leacock! By pointing out the value of women's skills, talents, and experiences, even after the traditional "womanly" roles had been fulfilled, McClung dealt a blow to any blanket use of that perpetual objection to woman's involvement outside the home. At least one modern critic, however, has interpreted the argument to mean that McClung thought that only mature women could move outside the home. "Even a suffragist as prominent as Nellie McClung, a temperance woman and a good representative of the social reform wave, could recommend careers only to women with grown-up children, women who had already fulfilled their maternal responsibility."[4]

But lest anyone now quote McClung in support of the theory that only single women, women like Hilda, and women with grown children could have careers outside the home, another short story needs to be told. (In all of this it can certainly be acknowledged that McClung personally valued her own roles as wife and mother very highly and always recommended the potential joys of those experiences. Children need nurturing and, given men's nature and nurture, she thought women were better equipped. Children might be most easily understood by their natural mothers, she thought, but she also thought that good and useful alternatives to this norm often made sense. It is all these alternatives which deny the stereotyped generalizations often made by modern critics.)

In a short story called "Every Woman Is Not A Housekeeper"[5] McClung described a family who made some creatively different decisions. Mrs. Frost, wife and mother, loathed housekeeping. Her loathing and inability combined with disastrous results; her frustration that she had so little time to help her children enjoy their school work completed her unhappiness. Aunt Ruth, the school teacher, had a magical hand with housework, but was prim, regular, and mechanical in her teaching. On one wet, gray day, when both women were particularly depressed by their jobs, they decided to switch places. The results delighted everybody. It was unanimously agreed that Mrs. Frost would take on the teaching position and Aunt Ruth would become the housekeeper. When asked his opinion, Mr. Frost just said, "Every lady to her liking..."

In all of this, Nellie McClung was fighting for a woman's right to define her own place and be responsible for her own choices. Why should women be restricted to a narrow little realm? "Women's place" and "women's sphere" were pretty familiar topics for writing and discussion in McClung's generation, but we have to realize that such terms depend on an understanding of the difference between men and women. What defines a woman's place as opposed to a man's?

One modern analyst, Elizabeth Janeway, produced this answer to that question: "what is male, according to prevailing distribution, is defined by 'world.' 'World' is man's place. Female is defined by a more restricted 'sphere' – woman's place. Women's place varies from society to society; it is whatever sector of man's world a given society has carved out for her."[6] In case that sounds like modern-day cynicism, compare it to what Nellie McClung wrote in 1915: "Man long ago decided that woman's sphere was anything he did not wish to do himself, and as he did not particularly care for the straight and narrow way, he felt free to recommend it to women in general."[7]

Her own life witnessed to her opinions. An article written for *Maclean's* in 1928 asked rhetorically: "Can a Woman Raise a Family and Have a Career?" It gave McClung a chance to state a resounding "yes" to that question, and to silence some opponents. She told an oft-repeated story about her youngest son Mark. With a rather wry whimsy, family members had taught the che-

Nellie with her granddaughter, Nellie.

rubic youngster to introduce himself as "Mark McClung, a suffragist's child who never knew a mother's love!" Obviously her family shared the awareness that their home life was under public scrutiny. In the same article, McClung wrote:

> I remember when the political fight in 1913 was raging and the Telegram, now defunct, was running cartoons of me every day, my youngest boy, three years old, ran away one morning and we were alarmed over his disappearance. But before we had time to be greatly disturbed, his brother, aged eight, delivered him at the back door, breathless with joy at being safe home with the young deserter. "I got him, mother," he shouted; "it's all right, the Telegram didn't see him; I sneaked him right up the lane."
>
> He would have made a more interesting picture for the Telegram than the weird things they were running, too, with his grimy little face, and one stocking at half mast.

From this and other comments, it seems evident that Nellie McClung was well aware of how careful she had to be in her public life, and that she was quite deliberate in the way she handled the potential for criticism from her contemporaries. Her own lifestyle was not exactly traditional. Her speaking tours frequently took her away from home. She knew that people might accuse her of neglecting her own home and family. During the height of her suffrage campaigning, she made a point of telephoning home before each lecture and then she would begin her address with words such as, "Settle down now and don't worry about my children. They are all well and happy, clothed and fed. The baby is in bed and all is well." It has been said that her five beloved children made her "vulnerable in five places."[8]

RESTRICTIVE LABELS

As I mentioned earlier, there has been debate over what kind of feminist McClung was. This may not seem very important unless we realize that the way we look at her feminism has a great deal to do with understanding her.

Let us look at a few more definitions. I offered a general definition of feminism: "the perspective which asserts the rights of women, critiques the ways in which those rights have been withheld or limited, and works to realize such rights fully." Linda Kealey, in her book *A Not Unreasonable Claim: Women and Reform in Canada, 1880s–1920s* states her working definition: "a perspective which recognizes the right of women not only to an increased public role, but also to define themselves autonomously."[9]

Kealey narrows down that definition, however, by using another term – "maternal feminism." She defines that as follows:

"Maternal feminism" refers to the conviction that woman's special role as mother gives her the duty and the right to participate in the public sphere. It is not her position as wife that qualifies her for the task of reform, but the special nurturing qualities which are common to all women, married or not. In some senses maternal feminism de-emphasizes or subordinates personal autonomy in favour of a (relatively) wider social role.

Because maternal feminists are seen to define themselves only in relation to someone else, what they could offer to ongoing feminist endeavors is often seen as severely limited. It can be charged that, as society gave women a slightly more public place, women simply broadened their understanding of the home that they should tend. Where once they had labored only in the most narrow of domestic circles, now they would be the housekeepers of the nation. A more constructive feminist approach, it is argued, would have challenged the very definition of women as housekeepers in the first place.

"Soft feminism" is another phrase that has been coined to describe the work of women who undertook new responsibilities – but only in areas which had traditionally been assigned to them such as among other women, the sick, and the disabled. Some people think that this kind of feminism was often encouraged by the church and in fact helped contribute to the development of maternal feminism.[10]

All of this has a lot to do with the way Nellie McClung has been seen in recent years. McClung has been labelled as a maternal feminist and therefore, I believe, underestimated. Modern historians argue that a fuller feminism based on natural rights quickly disappeared in Canada because of "the onslaught of maternal feminism."[11] Maternal feminism, therefore, becomes the wet blanket that smothered the sparks of a revolutionary fire.

The term "maternal feminism" has some usefulness but it certainly does not adequately describe McClung. Some of what she wrote may have fit the label, but the contradictory parts have been pretty much ignored. It is obvious that McClung wanted women to define their own place, and not just in relation to husbands or children!

One of the strong modern criticisms of earlier female reformers is that by emphasizing motherhood they did not change the traditional feminine role. One writer commented, "The conservative assumptions behind this argument are made explicit by Nellie McClung, who stated: 'Women are naturally guardians of the race, and every normal woman desires children.'"[13]

That quote was used with no mention made of its source or context. The sentence came from *In Times Like These* and was part of a chapter sardonically entitled "What do women think of war? (not that it matters)." The preceding chapter had expressed McClung's frustration with the warring spirit of men. She made it quite clear that women had to be the guardians of the race, because men had been bred to be warriors. She based that assertion on both nature and nurture. Men seemed to be inclined toward more aggressive behavior, but they had also been carefully taught. The jobs for women and men had been organized: "Men fought and women worked. Men fought because they like it, and women worked because it had to be done." McClung expanded on the theme.

> The masculine attitude toward life was: "I feel good today; I'll go out and kill something." Tribes fought for their existence, and so the work of the warrior was held to be the most glorious of all, indeed, it was the only work that counted. The woman's part consisted of tilling the soil, gathering the food, tanning the skins and fashioning garments, brewing the herbs, raising the children, dressing the warrior's wounds, looking after the herds, and any other light and airy trifle which might come to her notice.[14]

McClung did see alternatives to this rule even though she realized that, as a woman, her opinion might not "matter." She believed that there was a "curative power" available, but she was not sentimental about the stubbornness of the human heart. In the same chapter which provided the quotation above, she wrote that humanity has always learned the hard way: "Christ realized that when he looked down at Jerusalem, and wept over it: 'O Jerusalem, Jerusalem, how often I would have gathered you, as a hen gathereth her chickens under her wings, but you would not.'" McClung reflected that little had changed in the ensuing generations: "Humanity has to travel a hard road to wisdom, and it has to travel it with bleeding feet."

To confine McClung to a stereotyped image of maternal feminism just does not reflect her accurately. She was battling popular wisdom which declared that women could not possibly raise children and be involved outside the home. Her resistance to narrowly assigned roles moved her to reject the premise that only one option could be handled. Why should women have to choose a single dimension of life?

SCRIPTURAL FOUNDATIONS

McClung was very aware how reassuring her own maternal image was to her contemporaries. That does not say that she was faking anything. Her home and family were immensely important to her. They were part of her reality and she showed astute perception for the political power that her maternal credentials brought.

She challenged the stereotypes of women in other roles as well as that of wife and mother. She had words to say too about women being perceived as "angels" and women who were "put on pedestals":

> Another shoot of this hardy shrub of prejudice is that women are too good to mingle in everyday life – they are too sweet and too frail – that women are angels. If women are angels we should try to get them into public life as soon as possible, for there is a great shortage of angels there just at present, if all we hear is true.

> Then there is the pedestal theory – that women are away up on a pedestal, and down below, looking up at them with deep adoration, are men, their willing slaves. Sitting up on a pedestal does not appeal very strongly to a healthy woman – and besides, if a woman has been on a pedestal for any length of time, it must be very hard to come down and cut the wood.

Nellie McClung's reflections on the passage of scripture where Jesus corrected his listeners as to the nature of his mother's blessedness (Luke 11:27–28) gives another glimpse of the kind of feminist she really was. McClung paraphrased the "Blessed is the womb..." wording to "Your mother is a blessed woman to have brought such a son into the world." Her exposition of the passage makes an important contribution to the whole discussion of her understanding of "woman's place":

> ... *Christ interrupted his lesson long enough to correct the impression which he knew was in her mind. He said to her: "Yea!" Agreeing with the tribute to his mother, but – now listen to his correction – "Yea, rather, blessed are they that hear the word of God and keep it." In these words Jesus wipes out the comparison of the sexes and puts women forever on the same footing as men, in their relation to God.*
>
> *He enunciates a great principle, which even the church ignored. No fulfilment of biological function, however important, no relation growing out of that fulfilment even to the motherhood of the Messiah can supersede the soul's responsibility to God.*[15]

McClung demonstrated too keen an insight into the power and politics of "woman's place" and presented too strong a challenge to be accorded the simple title of "maternal feminist" with its attendant limitations. Her feminism, moreover, was so interwoven with her religious perspective and her own theological framework, that the two can not be separated.

CONCERT

The ladies of the Presbyterian church will give a Concert in Reid Hall,

ST. VINCENT, MINN.

Thursday Evening, Dec. 2nd.

Mrs. Nellie L. McClung, one of the leading entertainers of Winnipeg, assisted by local and neighboring talent, will render the program.

Refreshments will be served at close of program.   Proceeds go to the church fund.
Admission, 35 and 25 cts.

CHAPTER 5

THE SOCIAL GOSPEL IN A FEMINIST VOICE

How very glad I would be to exercise my religion in a peaceable, blameless, mellow way; to sing hymns, read my Bible, teach dainty little dimpled darlings in Sunday school, carry Jellies to the sick, entertain strangers, and let it go at that. Then I would have the joy of hearing people say, "She is a very sweet woman."

But here is the trouble. God demands our love, not just our amiability. [1]

Nellie McClung wrote those words in 1942, as she began the last decade of her life. But there is ample evidence that she had lived all her years under the same belief. Even these few words reveal something of her theology.

McClung had a deep and persistent faith in God and was always committed to, and involved in, her church. She was a staunch Methodist who supported the proposal for union and became an enthusiastic member of the new United Church in 1925. Anyone would acknowledge that she was a woman of deep religious faith, but we need to know more about her theology, and her theological perspective, to understand her work.

As the last chapter showed, McClung's feminism was a motivating force in her efforts. But beyond that, always, her commitment to her faith was a primary motivation. Sometimes the two were not easily compatible. It is just as important for us to know the context of her faith as it was to determine the context of her feminism.

Let us begin by identifying some of the beliefs she held.

God was no distant, removed, uninvolved deity for Nellie McClung. In her words, "God did not make the world and then retire to a Great White Throne to watch the people he made killing each other."[2] God was One to obey and to follow but also One to be engaged and questioned. McClung could firmly state that "listening and obeying the small voice...

not telling God what he ought to do with the troublemakers... listening and then following" was the task for Christians. One day each person would have a chance to meet God face to face, she believed, but until then God's presence could be known in day-to-day living. She cheerfully admitted that she did have questions and she would ask them at her first opportunity!

> I have a few questions I will ask if happily I arrive at the heavenly country. No doubt there will be certain days set apart when a private member can interrogate the Government. Especially do I want to know how it is that a just God has allowed the sins of the fathers to be visited on the children. Even the virtues of the mothers, inherited by the same law, do not balance the account. I will ask about these and other things, and in the meantime I am ready to believe that God is in his heaven, and is not overlooking anything.[3]

That passage illustrates McClung's mixture of direct and, probably unintentionally, convoluted reflections. Her reading of "sins of the fathers" as exclusively referring to men carries no shades of irony; present-day proponents of inclusive language could find a degree of hilarity in that! Her sentiment that God is not "overlooking" anything also carries a potential, but surely unintentional, double-entendre. After all, her words were not meant to be a theologically profound comment!

McClung was also sure that here was a "future state... a land where the complications of this present world will be squared away. Some call it a Day of Judgment; I like best to think of it as a day of explanations. I want to hear God's side."[4] This talk of heaven, however, did not imply that McClung was preoccupied by other-worldly hopes. On the contrary, she wrote that too often people ignored their world and all its needs because of vague hopes of heaven. The church should teach such folk better, she cried:

> The church must renounce the idea that, when a man goes forth to preach the Gospel, he has to consider himself a sort of glorified immigration agent, whose message is, "This way, ladies and gentlemen, to a better, brighter, happier world; earth is a poor place to stick around, heaven is your home." His mission is to teach his people to make of this world a better place – to live their lives here in such a way that other men and women will find life sweeter for their having lived. Incidentally, we win heaven, but it must be a result, not an objective.[5]

CONSISTENT JUSTICE

Along with this, McClung held that the emphasis should not be on individual salvation: "The church has directed too much energy to the business of showing people how to die and teaching them to save their souls, forgetting that one of these carefully saved souls is after all not worth much." People should, instead, remember Christ's injunction to lose their lives for Christ's sake, that they might find life. In McClung's words, "the soul can be saved only by self-forgetfulness."[6]

Nellie McClung at about 70 years of age.

McClung believed strongly that the prophetic call of God required justice instead of burnt offerings, and action instead of pious but empty sentiments. In one of my favorite speeches she declared, "Too much of our well-wishing has expended itself in wishing. Too often have we had the spirit of the Southern Colonels, who, after their banquet, which had been a feast of wine and song, felt so exalted in heart, that they wanted to do something to make all the world brighter and happier. Many ways were discussed but did not seem practical. At last one of the company had a brilliant idea. 'Let us,' he said, 'give three cheers for the poor.'"[7] Unfortunately, "well-wishing" was just not good enough.

McClung assumed that religious and secular thought were linked together and both her life and her words reflected that perspective. A newspaper article called her one of "... a growing group of Canadian men and women" who were demanding that "Christianity bear some real relation to the professions embodied in its teachings." The article said that these people had finally broken with what H.G. Wells had called a "muffled Christianity" which aimed for a "mist of finer feelings" but wanted no inconvenience or upset in the concerns of social or business life. In contrast, McClung and others, while applauding dignity in the church, also called for dignity in ordinary life, dignity in the field, the factory, the office and the store, and dignity in the affairs of big corporations.[8]

Her perspectives on Christianity peeled open the often contradictory practices of so-called Christian nations, in their efforts to advance their commercial interests. McClung perceived and condemned the hypocritical self-serving which frequently hid behind the skirts of missionary zeal.

> *Take the case of the heathen – the people whom we in our large-handed, superior way call the heathen. Individually we believe it is our duty to send missionaries to them to convert them into Christians. Nationally we send armies upon them (if necessary) and convert them into customers! Individually we say: "We will send you our religion." Nationally: "We will send you goods, and we'll make you take them – we need the money!" Think of the bitter irony of a boat leaving a Christian port loaded with missionaries upstairs and rum below, both bound for the same place and for the same people, both for the heathen "with our compliments."[9]*

SERMONS IN DISGUISE

McClung did think that constructive change could begin quite simply. People could be influenced towards good by teaching and by example. These perspectives pervaded her stories and novels. They are particularly apparent in the last two of her three Pearlie Watson novels: *Sowing Seeds in Danny, The Second Chance, Purple Springs*.

The novels are full of incidents where children contribute the clear-eyed perspective which allows a transgressor to confront his or her wrongdoings. On repeated occasions it is Pearl's impromptu prayers which precipitate change; in one such passage Pearl tries to encourage a young doctor who has lost his nerve to operate immediately on a critically ill man. Even a scrap of her dialogue gives you the idea: "O God, dear God," she prayed, beating her hard little brown hands together, "don't go back on us, dear God. Put the gimp into Doc again; he's not scared to do it, Lord, it looks like it, but he isn't. You can bank on Doc, Lord, he's not scared. Bear with him, dear Lord, just a minute – just a minute – he'll do it, and he'll do it right. Amen."[10]

In the story, the doctor performed the operation successfully and said in retrospect, "The bravest little girl in all the world was here and shamed me out of my weakness and," he added reverently, "I think God himself steadied my hand."

Whenever people behaved ignobly, they were to be challenged with the confidence that they could change: "You are young yet, and your life is all before you, and you must repent and begin all over again. 'While the lamp of life holds out to burn, the vilest sinner may return.'"[11] In stories such as these, advice for change usually accompanied the charges of wrong-doing. There was usually some down-to-earth suggestion for "making things right." It was understood that children had much to teach adults, and that children themselves only needed to receive proper nurturing to realize their full and honorable potential.

Again, there was that explicit confidence that God was actively involved in humanity's living and dying. So pervasive was this belief in Nellie McClung's novels that one reviewer in 1943 declared that McClung's "didactic enthusiasm" had marred her art. "Some of her stories," he wrote, "are sermons in the guise of fiction." McClung recounted this in her second autobiographical volume and unrepentantly declared, "I have never worried about my art... and if some of my stories are, as Mr. Eggleston says, sermons in disguise, my earnest hope is that the disguise did not obscure the sermon."[12]

Nellie McClung cheerfully made God a central figure in many interchanges. Although the incidents varied a great deal, there was often little point other than that of showing a God who was actively involved with creation. An editorial on thrift which appeared in the *Canadian Home Journal* in September 1916 provides one example. McClung wrote that a little girl had once questioned her mother about the creation of the animals she had seen at a circus. "Did God make elephants?" she asked. Assured that God had, she went on to ask about the rhinoceros, tigers and lions. "And then who made the butterflies?" she persisted. Told that God had made them too, the little girl responded, "Well, I hope he made the butterflies first, for after he had been making all those big things, butterflies would seem to be a pretty fiddlin' job!"

AGONIZING OVER WARS

When war came, Nellie McClung expressed deep distress over its incredible waste. She was not strictly a pacifist – though some of her statements carried those overtones. War was the symptom of the world's disease, she once wrote – "the withering, blighting, wasting malady of hatred, which has its roots in the narrow patriotism which teaches people to love their own country and despise all others."[13] Nevertheless, with the first World War underway and one of her own sons, a "sunny-hearted lad," transformed into a soldier, "a man of hate, a man of blood,"[14] McClung addressed herself to hopes that the war would eventually provide some benefit and that lessons would be learned from even the horrors. She may even have convinced herself that it was a necessary evil, if only to give herself a way of enduring those years.

An article written by McClung at the time of the second World War illustrates the mix of thoughts and emotions which characterized her troubled mind. She asked: "Can we combine the love of God with the killing of men? Can we say, 'Forgive us our trespasses as we forgive them who trespass against us,' and then proceed to bomb our enemies?" She pondered her own questions: "There was a time when I was much troubled over these things. Mahatma Gandhi says the English people should not resist Hitler, but let the Germans come and live in their big houses. Nonresistance, he says, will end the war. That may be so, but it will not bring peace, or freedom."[15]

She was still caught by conflicting thoughts. She said that she could see some benefits in this "episode" on the "march toward civilization": "We are better citizens than we ever were, and better Christians." She argued that the latter was true because "even the most remote, long-distance Christian" was being forced to reflect on the meaning of faith. Religion was being called to give up its "memorial flavor" and become "more vital and of a tougher fibre."

This sturdy optimism, however, was counterpointed by her sense that war poisoned everything. Literally in the midst of her article, with all its sturdy assurances, were sentences revealing her own emotional turmoil: "My worst time is when I wake. The blackness of the pit rolls over me then. All the horror, cruelty and suffering of the world consumes me like a hot blast from hell."

A SENSE OF MISSION

Over the years McClung kept promoting the need for financial support of mission work. In 1912 she wrote the preface to "Organized Helpfulness," the report for 1911–12 of All People's Mission in Winnipeg. A review in a local newspaper hailed her contribution and said that she "sounded the key-note of the mission" when she wrote:

> The missionary spirit in our churches is changing, evolving, advancing... To clothe the poor has ceased to be our highest conception of our duty to our neighbor, for somehow the idea has been borne in upon us that our neighbor, poor though he may be and ignorant and "foreign," is a man of like passions as ourselves, and that old clothes alone will never satisfy the hunger of his heart, nor clear us of our responsibility. What he needs is just what we need – it is understanding,

fellowship, companionship – the human touch. Absent treatment and long-distance methods cannot be effectively used in missionary work.[16]

In an article published in 1937 she wrote about a sermon she had heard which portrayed Jesus as the great disturber – "the One who will not let us fall into materialism, or be satisfied with narrow patriotism, or things of second-rate importance."[17]

She echoed that theme in a pamphlet published that same year by the Board of Home Missions for the United Church of Canada. She called for greater support of the church's work both in the expenditure of time and money: "Religion may have grown cold and formal in carved pews and high vaulted cathedrals, but not on the mission fields where the need is great and men and women are hungry. There are no theological differences there, no hairsplitting." In 1941 she suggested that the church was suffering from difficulties akin to those of the rich man of whom Christ spoke. "Most of us are too sleek and contented, our muscles too soft from inaction to get into active service for God."[18] Time and again she reiterated that "fat cat" existence was not life as God had given it. She wrote a poem entitled "A Prayer for the New Year" which indicated that, to her, such an existence was not living at all:

> *Lord, let me live while I can see*
> *The message in the blossoming tree;*
> *The beauty in the wayside flower,*
> *And love it for its one short hour;*
> *While morning song of lark and jay*
> *Can scatter all my doubts away,*
> *And lift my poor heart from the sod,*
> *And tell me I am Born of God!*
> *While I can feel I'm linked with all*
> *The burdened ones who halt and fall;*
> *While I can feel my share of shame,*
> *In every cheek that's dyed with shame*
> *While I can feel life's burdens sweep*
> *Across my heart, and drive out sleep;*
> *While I can hunger, suffer, strive,*
> *Lord, let me live – for I'm alive.*
>
> *But if the time shall come when I*
> *Forget to lift my eyes on high,*
> *Forget to seek for love divine,*
> *Or seek it, but for me and mine;*
> *When my dim eyes shall fail to trace*
> *Thine image in each human face;*

When, lulled by comfort, ease, or pride
I find my soul is satisfied,
To build its house of wood and hay
And let the old world go its way;
Content to preen before a glass,
While wounded ones, barefooted, pass
Easing my conscience, when I must,
By throwing hungry dogs a crust,
Then, Lord, thy crowning mercy shed,
And let me die – for I am dead.

Although her support and work for the church never faltered, McClung did express disappointment about her church's limitations. She wrote once that sincere critics had called the church the police dog of Capitalism, defender of the powerful and best friend to the controlling interests. In her opinion the church hadn't always been the outspoken advocate of fair play and justice that it might have been. But she argued that, as with most things, there had been a reason: "the church has needed the protection, the support of the state, or thought it needed it."[19]

SIGHT FOR BLIND EYES

Her sharpest criticism, however, was leveled at the church for its failure to show leadership in the advancement of women's issues and women's rights. McClung felt that it had been "strangely blind" in its attitude toward women and was convinced that many women would hold bitter memories of the church's immobility when asked to act. Even the governments of the western provinces had given equality to women before the church, she declared.

Challenged that few women expressed as much concern as she did for rights within the church, she retorted: "It is quite true that the women of the church have not said much, for the reason that many of the brightest women, on account of the church's narrowness, have withdrawn and gone elsewhere, where more liberty could be found." While their departures were understandable, McClung said it would have been far better to have "stayed and fought it out than to go out slamming the door."[20] That was the policy she herself adopted. Though she was more than once tempted to slam doors too, she did choose to "stay and fight it out" – even though her feminism often exposed a side of her church that she did not like. That is particularly clear in her work for the ordination of women.

Feminism, discussed in the preceding chapter, also shaped her interpretation of scripture. She perceived injustice and chauvinism in many commonly accepted passages. She told her readers how Jephtha (Judges 11) had vowed he would sacrifice the first living thing that came out to meet him, if the Lord would give him victory over the children of Ammon. When his only daughter came out to welcome him home, he kept his vow. As McClung said, pointedly, the story carries no word of censure. Jephtha was a "man of valor." Nellie concluded:

> *The last verse of the chapter says the daughters of Israel made a pilgrimage of four days every year, to lament the daughter of Jephtha. I would like to see the unexpurgated minutes of that four-day Convention, but I can imagine what the women thought of the "valiant" man who paid his vow by slaughtering his daughter.* [21]

Not only did her feminism affect her reading of scripture, but it also affected McClung's understanding of Christianity as a whole. Even while she continued to be a committed Christian herself, she was aware that Christianity had sometimes been used against women. As she once wrote: "The tragedy of the 'willing slave, the living sacrifice,' naturally does not strike a man as it does a woman."[22] On another occasion she declared: "Suffering, sacrifice, service – these three were women's undisputed domain... And so sure was the belief that women should suffer, that not so very long ago there were protests in a Christian church against the use of chloroform in childbirth as being unscriptural. The curse of Eve must not be set aside!"[23]

In McClung's opinion, the problems lay not in Christianity and its lessons, but in the manipulation of that material by people who wanted Christianity to serve their own ends. She was quite pointed in her remarks: "Christ taught the nobility of loving service freely given; but such a tame uninteresting belief as that did not appeal to the military masculine mind. It declared Christianity was fit only for women and slaves, whose duty and privilege it was lovingly to serve men."[24] This had, to McClung's mind, obvious consequences for women's participation in the church.

It is interesting to compare McClung's insights with those of a well-respected modern theologian. Letty Russell has written: "It is simply *not* Good News to someone trying to break out of the 'servant class' to hear that God has called her to be a servant!"[25] In Russell's opinion this is, however, a dilemma which must be faced and lived with; it is a central teaching of the Gospel even though its meaning has been abused throughout history.

As women we are confronted with the word "ministry" *(diaconia)* and its meaning of servanthood. As Christians we cannot avoid the word, in spite of its symbolic oppressive overtones. But, Russell says, the word servant in the Gospel does not mean that Christians of any race, sex, or class are condemned by any other oppressing groups to inferiority. "Regardless of what the role of servant has come to mean in the history of the church and society, in the Bible it is clearly a role of privilege and responsibility to take part in God's work of service in the world. Women and men are called by God in Jesus Christ to be both servants and apostles."

THE "SOCIAL GOSPEL" CONTEXT

Tempting as it might be to consider Nellie McClung's faith only from our modern perspective, it is important to understand her own context before we make too many leaps into our own day. McClung's beliefs were shared by many of her generation. A movement which came to be known as the Social Gospel reflected much of the same faith stance, though McClung did bring new dimensions to the mainstream of that movement in her identity as a woman and a feminist. In other words, her theology

was a typical product of the Social Gospel, while at the same time it carried strong features born of another parent, feminism.

The term "Social Gospel" will not be familiar to everyone. Compared with the accounts of the Social Gospel movement in the United States, there have been relatively few works by Canadian authors on the Canadian version of the same movement. There are, however, several very helpful and concise contributions to the discussion which can give us an outline or a framework for our understanding. A good start might be a working definition, from Richard Allen in his book *The Social Gospel in Canada*:

> The Social Gospel that arose in the latter years of the 19th century... developed under influences which encouraged a social concept of man and underlined the social dimensions of the Gospel, so that the solutions that appeared to be most useful were those which had an essentially social character. The Social Gospel addressed the whole problem, not just of individuals, not just of informal social groups, but of institutions and institutional relationships in society. Therefore, it became very deeply involved in virtually every promising reform of the time. The Social Gospel was not just incidentally social religion, people in its ranks could be heard muttering that the real holy communion, after all, did not take place in the church but was celebrated daily in the homes and farms and workshops of the nation.[26]

Instead of intensely individualistic conceptions of humanity and society, therefore, this "social" understanding of the gospel addressed humanity's problems from a much wider perspective. You can see how this perspective appeared in McClung's own thinking.

McClung was generally consistent with the Social Gospel movement in her understanding of a God actively involved with humanity, her conviction that the church's emphasis should not be on individual salvation, and the inter-connectedness of her economic, social, political and theological views. Faith was to issue in action; that conviction produced a strong sense of mission centered more on justice than charity. She shared the movement's optimism about reconstructing society based on democratic Christian principles, its international outlook and its ecumenical spirit. Her work with the League of Nations and her efforts towards church union were also consistent. She too believed that children were born pure and not evil and that teaching and example would influence people towards good.

Although McClung had much in common with the Canadian Social Gospel movement, she did not deliberately try to follow that trend. In an article entitled "What Religion Means To Me," she candidly declared: "I have never been much of a theologian. Doctrinal discussions have a moldy taste and are dusty to the palate. I believe we all know enough to live by. It is not so much spiritual food we need as spiritual exercise." Though there was consistency to her religious sentiments, there is no sign that she ever tried to construct a clearly defined and articulated theology. Rather, she delighted in presenting what was hailed as down-to-earth wisdom and grassroots biblical interpretation.

McClung was not the only one to think that spiritual exercise was important. An American theologian, Walter Rauschenbush, once said, "We select those theoretical ideas which agree with our experience and are cold to those which have never entered into our life."[27] McClung too was quite cold to theoretical principles which did not affect her life.

Instead, Nellie McClung's faith always served as the ground of her being. She certainly found a degree of companionship in the pervasive movement of the Social Gospel, but she also added her own contributions because of her feminist passion.

We do not have to defend her contribution to Canadian church and social life by arguing that she made her contribution in a unique theology – only that her theology was integral to her action and agitation for change. All reflection that we do on her life, her writing, and activities, must be done in the light of her Christian faith.

CHAPTER 6

AN APOSTLE OF UNREST

To bring... about... the even chance for everyone... is the plain and simple meaning of life. This is the War that never ends. It has been waged all down the centuries by brave men and women whose hearts God has touched...

To this end let us declare war on all meanness, snobbishness, petty or great jealousies, all forms of injustice, all forms of special privilege, all selfishness and all greed. Let us drop bombs on our prejudices! Let us send submarines to blow up all our poor little petty vanities, subterfuges and conceits, with which we have endeavored to veil the face of Truth. Let us make a frontal attack on ignorance, laziness, doubt, despondence, despair, and unbelief!

The banner over us is "Love," and our watchword "A Fair Deal." [1]

If this was war, then Nellie enlisted as a youngster. She had a crusading spirit even in her childhood. Even though hindsight often has an effect on autobiography, it is still interesting to read about Nellie's own account of her early interest in justice issues. In her book *Clearing in the West*, the first volume of her own story, she recalled several incidents in her childhood and youth which give vivid glimpses of her fledgling political consciousness and her first realizations that she, as a female, would have difficulty finding a hearing for her opinions.

One story revolved around the family's Christmas celebrations the year Nellie Mooney was 12.[2] A neighboring family had joined them for their hearty dinner of turkey and plum pudding. After dinner the men sat and talked of the "trouble Louis Riel was causing." The women listened as they washed dishes. The adults were anxious to have the trouble resolved. They thought that a good show of force by the government would end the problem.

Young Nellie badly wanted to speak. She had learned in school that there were good causes for the Indian and Metis grievances and strongly disliked the tone of the conversation but was afraid to cause trouble for her teacher if she did manage to make her opinion known. It was her older sister, Hannah, who first voiced a contradictory position and because she had a "quiet and dignified way of expression" and seldom spoke out, she surprised the adults into listening to her. Nellie later reflected that their mother would have known what to do with her youngest child, but this generally serene older daughter, the image of her own mother, caught her speechless!

Hannah, once she had spoken her piece, retired from the conversation, but Nellie feared that a "hostile tide of opinion gathering and sweeping ahead of it all good sense and reason" could result in her teacher losing his job. Enlisting the help of her beloved oldest brother, Will, to gain the attention of her parents and their friends, Nellie made her own plea for understanding. Making a strategic retreat from the room as soon as she finished speaking, she did not hear until later how her speech had been received. Her sister informed her that Will had just laughed and said they put their case well, but their mother put them in the same class as Guy Fawkes, the English conspirator who had been executed for his part in the plot to blow up the British Houses of Parliament in 1605. Mrs. Mooney was determined to go to the school trustees herself to complain. Her mother, Nellie said, had "the old-world reverence for men" and very clear ideas about "woman's place." Nellie was anxious for weeks about her mother's threat to complain until a "good will" visit from the school teacher ended the hostilities.

AN EXPERIENCE OF DISCRIMINATION

Another incident occurred when McClung was 18 and teaching at Hazel school near Manitou, Manitoba.[3] A Mrs. C.H. Brown had persuaded Nellie to attend a political meeting. Mrs. Brown said that Nellie had shown an "original cast of mind" in her teaching and discipline at the school. Although she usually found it hard to rouse women, she thought Nellie showed promise. It was a man's world, Mrs. Brown said, and women needed the vote because of the existing laws. McClung wrote that she protested that there were compensations for women – that they led a more sheltered life – but Mrs. Brown reminded her that homes pass and husbands die.

According to McClung's accounts of that night, the speaker, the Honorable Thomas Greenway, had commented on the appearance of the two women and said he was glad to see them in the audience. "Politics," he declared, "concerned women as much as men, though he did not think women would ever need to actually take part in politics. But their influence was needed and never more so than at this time." McClung commented, rather sarcastically, that he had added, "It was the woman's place to see that their men folk voted and voted right and this he said (so even we could understand), meant voting Liberal; which brought applause from the audience."

During the evening, when a collection was taken to defray expenses, Nellie and Mrs. Brown put two neatly written and signed questions on the plate along with their contributions. They asked: "Are you in favor of extending the Franchise to women? If so when may we expect to have this privilege?" and "Are you in favor of women having homesteading rights, and if so, will you ask the Dominion Government to consider this?"

The chairperson of the evening noticed the women's pieces of paper and read them.

At this point McClung's ac-

Nellie McClung, Dec. 1910, Toronto.

counts differ. In 1929 she wrote that the chairperson showed it to a "supporting brother who sat beside him" and that they then "glanced darkly and disapprovingly" at the women before pocketing the questions. Mr. Greenway knew nothing about this, she said: "I know he would have answered the questions, honestly, but he did not get a chance."[4] In her autobiography published in 1935, however, she wrote:

> We saw the chairman read the questions and show them to Mr. Greenway, who laughed good-naturedly when he read them and looked down at us with a sort of fatherly rebuke in his eyes!... Then there were more whispers, the other speaker was consulted and he took the questions, read them, and shook his head. Then the chairman put the paper in his pocket, from which it was never recovered and we were sorry then that we had given our two quarters.

The discrepancy is interesting, but we can only speculate whether it was a deliberate political move on Nellie's part or not. Perhaps in the first accounts, she was being careful not to stir up trouble. In any case it is apparent that the incident made a lasting impression. She said herself that it did much to confirm her "feminist tendencies."[5]

A CRUSADING SPIRIT

Nellie McClung kept the same crusading spirit throughout her life. She continued to believe that life, "... the real abundant life of one who has a vision of what a human soul may aspire to be,"[6] had to be treated as a great struggle, as a war waged against ignorance, selfishness, prejudice and cruelty. This was the warfare upon which nations should concentrate their energies, not the stylized murder of one set of human beings by another. She believed that God willed justice and equality for all and the failure to have that will realized was humanity's responsibility.

Because she had such a strong sense of God's will for humanity, she felt equally sure that she had to contribute what she could to the fulfilling of that will. If everybody didn't understand this as clearly as she did, then she would just have to get them moving in the right direction!

There is always danger in attaching one label to a person but the word "agitator" describes at least part of what Nellie McClung was. Although she always showed as much affection for labels such as "mother" or "cake-baker" as anything else, few of her contemporaries would have disagreed that she stirred things up. "Agitator" is even an appropriate term, because one of the dictionary definitions is "an apparatus for shaking or stirring, as in a washing machine"[7] – an appropriately domestic touch! Combine that with the more usual political associations of the word, and we have a nice blend of Nellie's domestic and political involvements.

McClung's activism was not an end in itself. Her actions came as a response to her convictions. Nevertheless, she did show a flair for "stirring things up" and sometimes she definitely enjoyed that ability. Fence-sitting was not her hobby. As she once candidly commented, "There is something wrong with a 'Neutral' every time. My own opinion is that 'Neutral' is just another name for 'Nut.'"[8]

She also thought that "neutrality" often masked a profound apathy. Too many people behaved like cats, McClung declared – giving in to the temptation to curl up where it was comfortable and to close their eyes to anything which might disturb their slumber. As she used to say, "disturbers are never popular – nobody ever really loved an alarm clock in action – no matter how grateful they may have been afterwards for its kind services!" She took this a step further: "It was the people who did not like to be disturbed who crucified Christ – the worst fault they had to find with him was that he annoyed them – he rebuked the carnal mind – he aroused the cat-spirit, and so they crucified him – and went back to sleep."[9]

McClung saw a clear pattern to follow in "the One who is the real disturber of this world" and she herself was frequently successful with her own alarm-clock imitation. She jangled others out of their apathy and provoked a response from previously disinterested people.

The Need for Agitation

Because society had "women's place" so neatly defined, challenges to that definition were either welcome or threatening; that depended on your point of view. Some writers have played down or overlooked how confrontational McClung often was, but that does a great disservice to her and to history.

Nellie McClung was an agitator because she knew she had to be one if things were going to change. For one thing, she knew that she was fighting a double standard which could very effectively cripple her work. She described this once in an article, after she had run for election in Alberta. One day before the election, a woman telephoned and asked McClung whether she believed every word of the Old Testament was directly inspired by God. The caller explained that the women of her Ladies' Aid would like to vote for McClung, but they had heard her say in a Bible Society address that she thought some of the characters in the Old Testament could not be defended. McClung had said that Elisha had shown a nasty bit of temper when he cursed the children who had annoyed him! The Ladies' Aid group was afraid that she was tainted with modernism.

McClung asked her caller whether her group had similarly ascertained the religious views of her male opponent. "Oh no!" her interrogator replied. "It is entirely different with men, the world expects more of women."[10]

With this sort of "logic" to deal with, Nellie McClung was well aware of the fine line she had to walk between upsetting challenge and reassuring compromise. If she pushed at the wrong time she would only alienate; if she failed to push at all she might miss an opportunity for change.

In all of it, she did, however, have strong feelings about people who did not "fight fair." It particularly enraged her to have people try to attack her through her children. She refused to repeat the sort of things that had been said but she said such attacks caused the one really sore spot in her public career. The fact that there were people mean enough to show hostility and spite to her children always made her angry. "That is the one part of my public life that has really hurt. You know the old saying: 'He who brings children into the world gives hostages to fortune.'"[11]

SYSTEMIC INJUSTICE

Nellie did not think that all problems were caused by individual people. The injustice she saw was not just a random collection of individuals' wrongdoings. She was well aware that the *status quo* was in place because of, and maintained by, broad social and economic forces. The system served parts of the society very well and those who profited did their best to see that things didn't change; hence "the war that never ends."

Nellie McClung directed her agitation at both individual and group targets. Although she was trying to motivate women to claim their individual rights to vote, hold office, preach, or in some other way live out their "personhood," she was well aware of the social impediments which were larger than any individual's own situation. Women had been kept preoccupied, she said with sympathy, and tiredness or distraction often prevented them from identifying their captivity.

Apathy from fatigue received very different treatment from McClung than the apathy which was bred by self-interest among "comfortable" women. Of the latter she wrote:

> The most deadly uninteresting person, and the one who has the greatest temptation not to think at all, is the comfortable and happily married woman – the woman who has a good man between her and the world, who has not the saving privilege of having to work. A sort of fatty degeneration of the conscience sets in that is disastrous to the development of thought... I believe God intended us all to be happy and comfortable, clothed, fed and housed, and there is no sin in comfort, unless we let it atrophy our souls, and settle down upon us like a stupor. Then it becomes a sin which destroys us. Let us pray:
>
> > From plague, pestilence and famine,
> > from battle, murder, sudden death,
> > and all forms of cowlike contentment,
> > > Good Lord, deliver us![12]

Some of McClung's most scathing words were directed at women who cultivated an identity she called the "gentle lady." These were the women, she said, who still believed in the "masculine terror of tears and the judicious use of fainting."[13] These Gentle Ladies did not want to hear distressing things – lest it make their heads ache and "when the Gentle Lady has a headache it is no small affair...!" These "Ladies" were particularly bitter against the militant suffragette, McClung asserted, because they could not understand her nobility of heart and unselfishness of purpose.

In contrast to this "cowlike contentment," however, was the apathy of exhaustion. "The horse on the treadmill may be very discontented," she declared, "but he is not disposed to tell his troubles, for he cannot stop to talk."[14] Similarly, women who had traditionally toiled from 5 a.m. to 5 p.m. had no time for thought or for gathering together. Some women were finding more leisure by this time, however, she said, and they were using that time to think. McClung wrote: "Factory-made articles have given them more time for thought, for social functions, for charity, for visiting the poor, the dying and the sad. They have been wondering about the underlying causes of poverty, sadness and sin."[15] These same women, she declared, now that they had time to reflect on their condition, were not willing to accept their "place" any longer – and they were creating a new (and to McClung, welcome) spirit of discontent.

That "spirit of discontent" really was the focus of Nellie McClung's most consistently witty and politically combative written work, *In Times Like These*, published in 1915. That work alone earns McClung a place as a feminist. Page after page, chapter after chapter, she pinned the oppressive domination of women to the wall for all to see. Even her contemporaries could sense its impact. One reviewer, when the book came out, called it a volume of protest. "It is the first considerable articulation in literature of the Western Canadian spirit of social reform... It is when Mrs. McClung turns her darts on the present status of women in society that she becomes a real apostle of unrest."[16]

Throughout that book, McClung named the discontents of women: discontent with their home relationships, with their church, with their country. That discontent could not be ignored any longer and, she added cheerfully, discontent had its positive side:

At the present time there is much discontent among women, and many people are seriously alarmed about it. They say women are no longer contented with woman's sphere and woman's work – that the washboard has lost its charm, and the days of the hair-wreath are ended. We may as well admit that there is discontent among women. We cannot drive them back to the spinning wheel and the mathook, for they will not go. But there is really no cause for alarm, for discontent is not necessarily wicked. There is such a thing as divine discontent just as there is criminal contentment. Discontent may mean the stirring of ambition, the desire to spread out, to improve and grow. Discontent is a sign of life, corresponding to growing pains in a healthy child.[17]

In spite of those reassuring words, however, McClung did not want the need for change to be underestimated. She wrote bluntly: "For generations women have been thinking, and thought without expression is dynamic, and gathers volume by repression. Evolution when blocked and suppressed becomes revolution."[18]

RESPONSE TO DISCONTENT

Political activism was the obvious step for discontented women to take, McClung argued. Certainly it could be seen as a natural outgrowth of religious commitment. In older days, McClung declared, God spoke by the mouths of prophets who administered the legal as well as the spiritual affairs of the state, so church tradition gave precedent to such political involvement.

She refused to accept a pietism which separated faith and works. Listing the social evils of prostitution, sweated industries and alcoholism, she insisted, "If we sit down under these things, gently acquiescent, we become in the sight of God a partner in them. Submission to injustice, submission to oppression is rebellion against God."[19]

"Revolution" or at least "revolutionary" is not too strong to describe the results that Nellie McClung helped to attain in two of her greatest efforts: suffrage, and the ordination of women in the United Church of Canada. A closer look at these issues and McClung's involvement reveals the contribution that her agitation made. Both involved levels of political activism. Both were connected in her mind. In fact, McClung expressed concern that the church's slowness to give women their rights would give fuel to the state's arguments against suffrage. She wrote that she was always afraid that she would be confronted in a public debate with the question, "If the church... with its spiritual understanding of right and justice, cannot see its way clear to give the vote to women, why should the State incur the risk?" That question, she said, was the graveyard past which she always had to whistle!

AGITATION FOR SUFFRAGE

Consider the struggle for the right of Canadian women to vote – perhaps we could say that it was the struggle for a seat. That would be in keeping with one of the word plays that McClung delighted in using during her many public speeches on the subject. Responding to opponents' charges that women wouldn't want to sit in parliament, she often quoted Dr. Anna Shaw's response: "... there are women who have stood before wash tubs and behind counters so long that they would be glad to sit any place."

Contrary to what one might expect, McClung spoke very warmly about the support the suffrage movement received from Canadian men. Although her arguments for suffrage were persistent and passionate, she always presented them as if everyone would see her points as obvious. That had the neat effect, of course, of making those who disagreed with her seem illogical and a minority! McClung did think, however, that Canadian women had less of a struggle than their British sisters. Generally speaking, she believed that Canadian men were more receptive to arguments such as hers.

McClung's work for suffrage in society and women rights in the church were often interwoven. One person has used the phrase "ecclesiastical suffrage"[20] to draw a parallel between the struggle in the church and that in secular society. The term works well to remind us just how closely the two were tied for Nellie McClung. In the years before Manitoba granted women suffrage, followed by the other provinces, McClung frequently spoke to both issues on the same occasions. Her arguments for both causes stemmed from the same conviction: that equal rights for men and women were God's will for humanity, and that it was illogical as well as unjust to deny that will its fulfillment.

Nellie McClung frequently expressed her surprise and dismay that some of the strongest opposition to suffrage had come from "religious" people. That could only be, she said, "a sad commentary on their failure to understand their Lord's plain teaching." Once again she quoted the passage (Luke 11:27–28) where Jesus corrected the supposition about his mother's blessedness and said that with those words Jesus wiped out the comparison of the sexes and put women forever on the same footing as men in their relation to God. As important as this passage of scripture was, she declared that in more than 40 years of regular church attendance she had never heard a sermon preached from this text.[21]

When writing and speaking, McClung often addressed the general question of women in politics because she felt that a more active role, including holding elected office, was as logical a consequence of secular suffrage as ordination was to ecclesiastical suffrage. She repeatedly argued that the change was inevitable. "People who deplore the entry of women into public life (and there are still some of them left), are too late now with their protests. The trouble began when women learned to read."[22] McClung also contradicted every claim that women were not meant to be involved in politics. Time and again she asserted that politics was nothing other than simple public responsibility:

Politics simply means public affairs, yours and mine, everybody's, and to say politics are too corrupt for women is a weak and foolish statement for any man to make. If he is in politics, it is an admission that he is party to the corruption or that he is unable to prevent it. And in either case something should be done. Men and women are one – indissolubly joined together for good or for ill, and what is too corrupt for woman is too corrupt for man. Women cannot escape corrupt social conditions by shutting their eyes.

Imagine a man taking his wife to a new home and telling her that the place was too filthy for her to live in, that she must remain upstairs; that the odors are bad, but that she can use her smelling salts, that nothing can be done toward bettering conditions.

That woman would tell her husband that his brain was skidding. Then she would purchase the strongest powder possible and clean that house.

Women have cleaned up things since time began; and if women get into politics there will be a cleaning-up of pigeon-holes and forgotten corners in which the dust of years has fallen.[23]

SADDENED AND DISILLUSIONED

McClung was absolutely sincere in such idealistic speeches. She was confident that women would use their votes to correct social ills. She was saddened and disillusioned when she had to acknowledge, late in her life, how much she had over-estimated the degree to which other women shared her ideals. Particularly offensive to her was the decline in temperance zeal:

...the battle for woman's emancipation, with its delegations, petitions, amendments, conventions... have taken years of my life and other women's lives but the center of gravity has shifted since then, and while I will not give way to regret that I spent so many years working for the equality of women, I cannot refrain from saying that the sight of women lined up in front of the Government Liquor Stores fills me with a withering sense of disappointment.

...Women could have sobered this country if they had willed it; that is a sore and withering thought. Why do we hold life so lightly? We, the women who pay for it with sweat, blood and tears?...

But these bitter observations had no part in our thoughts while we were waging the battle for what we called the emancipation of women.[24]

Publicly, however, there is no sign that McClung let this disappointment sour her enthusiastic calls to women to make responsible use of their new power. In a speech to a United Farmers of Alberta convention, she declared that unless enfranchisement, the right to vote, made life easier and safer for every woman, then women could feel they had failed. But, she said, she was sure that this would not be the case.[25]

Nellie McClung's agitation for suffrage always included arguments directed at any who opposed such a right. She addressed specific exhortations to women to rouse themselves to fully exercise their humanity. Her battles with the Roblin government in Manitoba attracted wide publicity, but she was just as challenging in her words to the women themselves.

She categorized three classes of women who, she said, did not want the vote:

(A) The good intelligent woman who hasn't thought about it – hasn't needed to – the woman who has a good man between her and the world, and who has never needed to go up against the ragged edge of things...

(B) The young woman who shrinks from being thought strong-minded, the frilly, silly, clinging vine – whose mental caliber is that of a butterfly – the girl who wants to be attractive to men, at any cost. This is a form of affectation which many of them outgrow...

(C) Class C is the selfish woman who does not care – who does not want to be bothered, the cat-woman who loves ease and comfort...[26]

McClung said that she would not attempt to categorize individual anti-suffragists, each was welcome to put on the cap that fit best. She added, however, that she did believe that 99 percent of women belonged to one of the first two categories and that their cases "were hopeful."[27]

UNCEASING PERSISTENCE

If McClung had been asked what was the most important ingredient in the struggle for suffrage she might well have said "persistence." Women tenaciously pursued their rights until they had them, but Nellie reminded them that the prejudice which blocked their efforts was incredibly resilient. "In regard to tenacity of life," she said, "no old yellow cat has anything on prejudice. You may kill it with your hands, bury it deep and sit on the grave, and, behold, next day it will walk in at the back door, purring!"

She continued: "The prejudices regarding woman suffrage have been blown to pieces many times. But they still exist. And men continue to do as they like and insist that every true, womanly woman should be at home with the nutmeg grater and the oiled mop."[28]

Although McClung remained a Liberal throughout her life, she frequently declared her dissatisfaction with party politics. Even when she was a member of the legislative assembly in Alberta she would not agree to follow party lines on all issues. As she wrote later, "I'm sure there were times when I was looked upon with disfavor. I could not vote against some of the... [opposing] measures, which seemed to me to be right and proper, and I tried to persuade my fellow members that this was the right course to pursue."[29] There are strong indications that Nellie thought that women's suffrage would bring major changes to the existing party system.

Nellie McClung believed that suffrage was women's right, but she also thought that increased activism of women might well be humanity's only hope. Appalled by the rupturing of the world by war, she wrote that the time had come to call out the "full force": "The women are our last reserves. If they cannot heal the world, we are lost, for they are the last we have – we cannot call the angels down... The trumpets are calling for healers and binders who will not be appalled at the task of nursing back to health a wounded world, shot to pieces by injustice, greed, cruelty, and wrong thinking."[30]

Such trumpets added further notes of urgency to the already important tasks of unsettling every injustice.

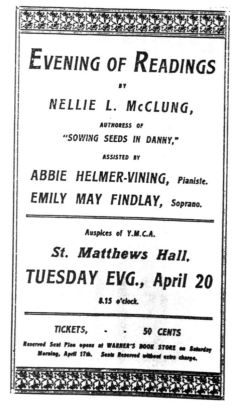

CHAPTER 7

PART OF A LARGER PATTERN

We may yet live to see the day when women will be no longer news! And it cannot come too soon. I want to be a peaceful, happy, normal human being, pursuing my unimpeded way through life, never having to stop to explain, defend, or apologize for my sex... I am tired of belonging to the sex that is called the Sex.[1]

This book focuses on the contribution made by Nellie L. McClung to her church and to Canadian society. We need to remember, however, that she was not alone in her work for change and justice. Although our history books have done a poor job of recording the work of women in our past, there are many exciting stories of the efforts of women to bring about a new reality for themselves. Nellie McClung would be among the first to stress the importance of keeping this perspective about the work she herself did.

To provide some of this context, let us take a look at a cause in which she was involved, but not as the major figure. The whole struggle came to be known as the "Persons Case." It is a fascinating illustration of the political climate for western Canadian women in the years immediately following the success of the suffrage movements in gaining the vote for women. The roots of the case were in the post-suffrage years and the case itself stretched over 13 years. The five main characters in the drama had all been trained in the atmosphere and experience of the struggle for the vote.

The Persons Case began with one particular individual and her question, but the outcome of the case affected all Canadian women.

EMILY MURPHY

The individual was Emily Murphy. Born Emily Ferguson in 1868 in Cookstown, Ontario, she was encouraged by her father to do all that her brothers did, although she often received her mother's criticism for her "tomboy" ways. Although she did not take the formal legal training given to her brothers, she showed her own flair for legal and political issues. She married Arthur Murphy, a young clergy person, when she was 19.

When Arthur's ill health necessitated a change, they moved to Manitoba.

Emily Murphy wrote during those years under the pen-name of "Janey Canuck" and that remained an affectionate term of address for her throughout the years. The Murphys moved on to Alberta in 1907 where Emily continued to write and also became very active in civic affairs. Among her efforts was work for temperance, suffrage, and Alberta's Dower Act, which ensured a certain proportion of a deceased husband's property for his widow.

THE CRUCIAL QUESTION

Emily Murphy was the person who asked the pivotal question: she asked whether the laws of Canada would acknowledge women as persons.

Where did such a question originate? Murphy's biographer has revealed that she found a note pinned to a Montreal letter of 1921 on which Emily had written: "How it all started." That is pretty conclusive evidence that she saw the letter to be a deciding factor in her decision to demand clarification of the legal understanding of "persons," but she had already had years of frustrating experience behind her to fuel the fires.

Five years earlier, for example, in 1916, a delegation from the Law Committee of Edmonton's Local Council of Women had arrived at the Guardroom of the North West Mounted Police to hear the evidence in a case charging some 20 young women with prostitution. The delegates had come to hear the evidence to make sure that the women were treated fairly. The Counsel for the Crown asked that they be made to leave because such cases were unfit to be heard in a mixed court. When telephoned for advice by the delegates, Emily Murphy told them to agree that the material was unfit for mixed company – and to call for a special court in which women offenders would be tried by a woman in the presence of women. To her amazement, the suggestion was accepted and she herself was made the first woman Police Magistrate. Within a year she had become Magistrate for the Province of Alberta.

Her first day brought the first challenge to her authority. She wrote:

My first day in court was as pleasant an experience as running a rapids without a guide... Presently all the men became embarrassed and started to stammer over their manner of addressing me. One said "Your Worship," and another "Your Honor." A negro said, "Your Majesty," and the rest said, "Sir." [2]

The day brought more than mere social awkwardness, however. Murphy was to hear a case involving a breach of the Liquor Act. The Counsel for the defense, Eardley Jackson, rose and objected to her jurisdiction as a magistrate. He argued that since *she was not a person* within the meaning of the Statutes she had no right to be holding court.

Jackson's objection recalled a decision of 1876 in the common law of England. A woman had decided to test the possibility of voting. She managed to persuade a poll clerk into giving her a ballot and then she cast her vote. As a result, she was arrested and tried and the ruling was made: "women are persons in matters of pains and penalties, but are not persons in matters of rights or privileges." Now that ruling was being recalled by Counsel Jackson to challenge Murphy.

The challenge was made repeatedly over the following years. While

Nellie McClung with Alice Jamieson (center) and Emily Murphy (right) in 1916. Jamieson and Murphy were the first women in the British Empire to act as police magistrates.

Murphy took a certain whimsical enjoyment out of having the whole argument repeated every time the objection was made, the situation also frustrated her deeply. A letter from her to a firm of Edmonton barristers in October of 1917 gives us a glimpse of her battle. On that occasion she wrote:

> *Sir,*
>
> *I am informed this morning in the Women's Police Court at the conclusion of the case of Rex vs. Nora Holt, you, in the presence of several persons, made use of the following grossly insulting words –*
>
> *"To Hell with Women Magistrates, this country is going to the dogs because of them. I would commit suicide before I would pass a sentence like that." Unless I receive from you an unqualified apology in writing, I shall regretfully be obliged to henceforth refuse you admittance to this Court in the capacity of Counsel.*
>
> *I have the honor to be, Sir,*
> *Your most obedient servant.*

A provincial court decision that women were not to be disqualified for such office calmed the situation in Alberta but that was not enough to close the issue.

Emily Murphy soon met the same problem again. As President of the Federated Women's Institute of Canada, she presided over a conference in 1919 which produced a unanimous resolution requesting the Canadian government to appoint a woman to the Senate. There is no evidence that she ever thought of herself for such a post until she received a letter from the Montreal Women's Club in 1921, asking permission to give her name as their nominee for the Senate. That was the letter to which her little note was pinned: "How it all started."

The Minister of Justice received the resolution but said that he did not believe women could be appointed because, within the meaning of the British North America Act, women were not persons. Murphy wrote to a friend that she just couldn't believe that here was more of the "same old rigmarole." The government changed and the resolution was resubmitted to the new Prime Minister, Arthur Meighen; the result was the same. William Lyon Mackenzie King was the third Prime Minister to be involved in the question when the death of an Albertan senator in February 1922 brought a new flood of appeals for Murphy's appointment. King expressed support and declared his willingness to seek an amendment to the Act, but no action followed.

It was Emily Murphy's brother, William, Mr. Justice Ferguson, who drew her attention to Section 60 of the Supreme Court Act which provided that any five interested persons could petition for an order-in-council directing the Supreme Court to rule on a constitutional point in the British North America Act. Murphy clarified and double-checked her interpretation of the section and learned that, in accordance with its provisions, the Justice Department had determined that the question was one of "sufficient national importance" to be presented and that the Department would pay "all reasonable fees" arising from the case, on behalf of the appellants. (Ironically, no one seemed to judge that the women weren't "persons" enough to present the question!)

THE OTHER FOUR

Having successfully made her application for permission to present such a petition she then proceeded to name her four other "interested persons." Nellie McClung appears to have been her first choice. The two women were close friends; McClung had gained a solid reputation for her wit, wisdom, imagination and determination in her work for suffrage and temperance. Hers was the most widely known name when she joined Murphy's battle and her reputation was a sizable contribution. In 1916, for example, a magazine article had hailed McClung as a "Joan of the West" and declared,

> No Canadian woman has spoken to both parts of the Dominion as she has spoken. Women from the motherland have come to Canada to advocate the cause of suffrage, but their words have not exactly fitted the case on this side of the water. The need was for the awakening of a consciousness of reform from within, and not so much for advice from without. Canada in this matter, as in others, was intended to work out her own destiny. And the need was for leadership. Western Canada has supplied a leader in Mrs. Nellie McClung.[3]

LOUISE MCKINNEY

The third name was Louise McKinney. A brief sketch of any of these women cannot do them justice, but it can perhaps give some feeling for the resources present in the five. Louise McKinney had been one of the first two women to be elected to a legislature in the British Empire; she was elected to the Alberta legislature in 1917 as one of the Non-Partisan League's two successful candidates. Particularly involved with the issue of temperance, she began her public career as a Women's Christian Temperance Union (W.C.T.U.) organizer and was president of the Dominion W.C.T.U. and vice-president of the World Union when she died in 1931.

Born in Ontario in 1868, she had received her education there, including her training as a teacher, but when she traveled to North Dakota to visit a married sister, she decided to accept a teaching position there. In 1896 she married James McKinney and together they returned to Canada in 1903 to homestead, part of the biggest wave of settlers to come into Canada from the south.

During her term in the Provincial House she held securely to her concerns for women and for prohibition. One of her most important legislative contributions was the introduction of a motion which led to the Dower Act. Modern reviewers would, of course, see her position as very traditional. Although she argued that women should have the right to define their own "sphere," she expected only one outcome. In her opinion, the average woman instinctively loved home life.

During her four years in office, the League was absorbed into the United Farmers of Alberta. McKinney disagreed with the new president's opinions, was defeated in the 1921 election and did not run again. Of her participation in this Case, the following has been said:

> In joining the progressive movement, Mrs. McKinney was carrying into the political sphere the crusading spirit of her temperance activities, only in this case the traditional political parties became the representatives of the "wealthy interests" that were enriching themselves at the expense of the farmer. Thus in Louise McKinney, Emily Murphy had a co-appellant who represented not only the Dominion-wide temperance movement, but the militant agrarian politics of Alberta.[4]

IRENE PARLBY

Murphy showed her consistent astuteness in her choice of the Honorable Irene Parlby as the fourth of the petitioners. Born in England in 1878, Irene Marryat spent her girlhood in India and Ireland and then on a visit to Alberta in 1896, married Walter Parlby.

Irene Parlby entered politics reluctantly, through her involvement with a local women's organization which sent her as a delegate to the United Farmers of Alberta (U.F.A.) convention in Calgary in 1916. She emerged from that convention as president of the women's branch. She resigned in 1918 but when she was urged to accept nomination in 1921 she agreed to run for the U.F.A. and won her legislative seat. Nellie McClung was also elected and it is recorded that the two women, though belonging to opposing parties, heard some unauthorized and unrecorded caucuses! McClung herself wrote that they were usually in agreement on matters affecting women.

Appointed to the Cabinet as Minister without Portfolio, Parlby wrote to another woman, declaring that her place was a "stupid position" because she was not officially responsible for anything in particular. Therefore, she unofficially assigned herself the portfolio of "women's lines of work." [5] During her 14 years in government, she worked on a variety of issues including health care services for rural communities, co-operatives, property rights of married women, and education.

Parlby's own experience probably prompted her quick acceptance of Emily Murphy's invitation. Sometime around 1935, in an article entitled "What Business Have Women in Politics?" she recalled that it was not until her first political campaign that she realized what "miserable incompetent creatures women were in the eyes of the public." She wrote: "I ought to have developed a terrible inferiority complex by the time it was over, for practically the only issue that seemed to concern the electorate or the opposition was that I was a woman, or worse, an English woman..." [6] It has been said, however, that as a member of the Alberta cabinet, Irene Parlby's participation as a co-appellant signified the support of the Government of the Province of Alberta, an important factor in securing the cooperation of the Government at Ottawa. [7]

HENRIETTA MUIR EDWARDS

Along with these three, Murphy selected Henrietta Muir Edwards as the fifth co-appellant. The most senior, Henrietta Muir was born in Montreal in 1849. She and her sister organized the Working Girls' Association in 1875, a forerunner of the Y.W.C.A., and edited *The Working Woman of Canada*, a periodical aimed particularly at social needs. She moved to Macleod, Alberta, after her marriage in 1886, and made her greatest, and longest, contribution through her work with the National Council of Women. She was convenor of its standing committee on laws, particularly as they affected women and children, for more than 35 years. Although she never had any formal legal training, she became an accepted authority and produced books on the legal status of women for both the Province of Alberta and for the Dominion of Canada.

THE CASE IS HEARD

These four women joined with Murphy to present their historic question: "Does the word Persons in Section 24 of the British North America Act, 1867, include female persons?" Sent in August of 1927, the case was not heard until March 1928. A known advocate of women's suffrage, the Hon. Newton Wesley Rowell argued the case for the five appellants. Because the case was concerned with the official interpretation of the B.N.A. Act, provinces were offered the opportunity of expressing their opinions. Only Alberta and Quebec spoke to the question: Alberta in support and Quebec against. (Women in Quebec did not get the provincial vote until 1940.)

Judgment was reserved for five weeks and then Murphy received Rowell's telegram of April 24, 1928: "Regret Supreme Court have answered question submitted to them in the negative."

Historian Catherine Cleverdon has since summarized the Crown's argument in five points.[8] First, it was claimed that any interpretation of the B.N.A. Act must have regard to the period when the Act was passed and new ideas should not be allowed to color the interpretation; no women were holding offices in 1867.

Second, the Act showed that it did not have any intention of including women by its use of masculine pronouns throughout, that in crucial sections the word "senatress" never appeared.

Third, women in 1867 were under every conceivable form of legal incapacity and barred from public functions so how could it be supposed that the drafters of the Act meant to include them?

Fourth, women were not permitted in the House of Lords so would it be reasonable to assume they were intended to sit in the Canadian upper house?

Finally, women had not held office in the provinces which confederated in 1867.

Mr. Justice Anglin, in his decision, concluded that while the word "persons" when used by itself, referred to all human beings, it was, in the Act, modified by words such as "fit and qualified" and carried the import that only men were eligible for appointment.

Emily Murphy and her co-appellants were very careful not to damage their chances at an appeal by making public denunciations of the Supreme Court decision. Others, of course, could be more free. Mary Ellen Smith, who had been a member of the British Columbia legislature, declared: "The iron dropped into the souls of women in Canada, when we heard that it took a man to decree that his mother was not a person." [9] Murphy's biographer has indicated that part of Murphy's care in selecting her group was a concern that each be able to speak to the issue but also that all would show wise judgment in their timing and choice of words.

When the government made no move to work for an amendment, Murphy forwarded her own petition for an appeal and when it was approved the question proceeded for decision to the Privy Council in London, England. Fearing that strong identification with British suffragettes at this point might harm their cause, Murphy reluctantly declined invitations to travel to England to listen to the case. Once again, Rowell presented the case, and the hearing began on July 22, 1929.

On October 18th the Lord Chancellor of Great Britain, Lord Sankey, read the Privy Council's verdict and thereby reversed the decision of the Canadian Supreme Court. Newspaper headlines proclaimed the victory: "Five Alberta Applicants Win Action"; "Canadian Women Beat Their English Sisters"; "Success in Canada May Influence Changes In House Of Lords." In reading the judgment, Lord Sankey stated that the exclusion of women from all public office was a relic of more barbarous days and that an appeal to Roman law, and to early English decisions, was not, of itself, a secure foundation on which to build an interpretation of the B.N.A. Act of 1867. Since, too, there were provisos in the Act which stipulated "male subjects," it could be understood that "person" was meant to be inclusive of both women and men.

Thirteen years after her identity as a person had first been publicly challenged, Emily Murphy received the news of the Privy Council's affirmative decision. Her biographer has said that at three o'clock that morning in her Edmonton home, Emily's daughter Evelyn was awakened

Lord Chancellor Sankey on his way to deliver judgment re "Persons." Oct. 18, 1929.

by the joyous calling of her mother. "Judge Murphy, in a white flannelette nightgown, her hair tousled, her cheeks flushed, was dancing with delight in the doorway. 'We've won! We've won!'"

THE AFTERMATH

It would be satisfying to end the story on such a note of elation. Certainly there was a great deal of celebration in the days which followed. Congratulations poured in. Reporters were quick to contact the appellants for their reactions and comments. The others of the five insisted that attention and gratitude should focus on Murphy.

Nellie McClung's press statement, quoted widely, called Murphy's handling of the whole case a "masterpiece of diplomacy." With the resolution of the case, all the women felt free at last to make more personal comments. Henrietta Muir Edwards was quoted in a newspaper as saying that this "marked the abolition of sex in politics." In an article published that December, McClung spent little time chastising the opponents of the decision and instead articulated her hopes for the future. It was at this time that she said she was tired of being part of "The Sex."

PAINS AND PENALTIES

Although the women maintained a strong public front, there is a poignant glimpse of their private experience in a letter from Emily Murphy to Nellie McClung in January, 1927. Murphy had been reading something which said that people should seek pleasure and avoid pain. At first, she said, she thought that was extremely selfish, but upon further reflection she thought that perhaps it did apply "to those of us who were past the first flush of youth and maybe were beginning to feel tired."[10] Perhaps she and Nellie erred in the opposite direction, she wrote. Perhaps the time had come when they owed it to themselves and their families not to seek pain but instead to "let themselves go to happiness." She knew that pain might come anyway but perhaps they could stop putting themselves deliberately in its way.

However, if removing themselves from public struggles was the remedy, neither of them took it!

After the Privy Council announced its decision, Prime Minister Mackenzie King was besieged by requests that Emily Murphy be appointed to the Senate, but when a woman was named at the end of 1930, the appointee was Cairine Wilson, a Liberal Party worker.

Once again, the five women showed impeccable discipline and graciousness, but there is evidence that at least Murphy and McClung were disappointed. Years later, in her autobiography, McClung's comment was still carefully worded. "It was a matter of regret for all of us that Mrs. Murphy was not appointed the First Senator, and that is no reflection on the excellent appointment that was made in the person of the Hon. Cairine Wilson."[11]

A letter, however, marked "private," from Murphy to McClung gives insight into their own thoughts on the issue. McClung had sent Murphy a clipping of a newspaper article which had lauded Wilson's appointment in place of one of the "industrious women politicians, spinsters, and others who have talked incessantly of their rights as women without discharging any of their responsibilities as such." Murphy commented: "Lord! I think we ought to ask now for an interpretation of the word 'responsibilities.'"[12]

The appointment may have been given more as a reward to Wilson than as a punishment for Murphy, but it would be difficult not to suspect retaliation against one who had so stirred the political waters. The next vacancy, during the government of R.B. Bennett, came with the death of a Senator from Edmonton, Murphy's home town. This time the requests for her appointment were denied on the grounds that recognition had to be given to the Roman Catholic minority. It was her last opportunity. Emily Murphy died in 1933.

An often quoted conversation that Lotta Dempsey, who had been Woman's Editor of the *Edmonton Bulletin* for many of those years of struggle, had with one of the senators from Edmonton adds what amounts to be an epigram.

"I wonder why they never did appoint Emily Murphy?" she asked.
The Honorable Senator spoke quickly, with deep conviction: "Oh we never could have had Mrs. Murphy in the Senate!" he said. "She would have caused too much trouble!"

PRESENT-DAY IMPLICATIONS

There has been time for more reflection since those first days of the aftermath – time to look again at the case and its implications. Renewed interest was generated by its 50th anniversary in 1979. For many Canadians, that was the first time we had even heard of it! *The United Church Observer* of October 1979 carried an article by Anne Squire which asked: "In 50 years, how much progress for women as 'persons'?" Citing the struggle women endured to be ordained, their exclusion by language and liturgy, the reluctance of parishes to have a woman person in the pulpit, and the many "congregations which do not encourage women to move out of the kitchen or beyond the choir, church school and U.C.W.," she concluded that "50 years later we must admit to them [the women's suffrage leaders] that there are still 'pains and penalties' in being a woman person in the United Church of Canada."[13] Obviously, the discussion did not end when Murphy's question was answered by the Privy Council.

Looking now at the biographies of those five women, we can see the scope and depth of the women's practical education. Temperance, suffrage, women's and children's rights, legal reform and involvement in the organization and leadership of powerful women's groups, were all areas engaged by the "Alberta Five." They had learned important lessons in those struggles.

When we reflect on the history of their struggle, helpful insights into contemporary issues can still be found. For example, one of the favorite techniques of oppression has long been to keep the oppressed occupied – and preoccupied! The pattern is reminiscent of fairy tales, in which a hero is given impossible tasks to complete – more correctly, it was always hoped that they were impossible! Women, in their struggles for freedom, have repeatedly experienced this same old dodge. Requirements are placed before them and when those are met, new impediments are added. Take an example from 1914. The Edmonton Equal Franchise League and the Local Council of Women of Calgary presented a woman suffrage petition to the Alberta government. It contained 12,000 signatures. Premier Arthur Sifton said that he would need proof of a more widespread demand!

Women were often instructed to attend to their "own concerns" as if those had no relevance or relation to the issues that the men were addressing. Nellie McClung was one who put her feelings about such treatment into words.

> *Recently when members of the W.C.T.U. went before our law makers in Ottawa, pleading for a much needed reform, the prohibition of cigarettes, pleading in the name of our boys, who are every day being ruined in body and soul, one of the members of Parliament rose in his place and told these women to go home and reform their own sex before they came looking for any reforms from men. He said women were the slaves of fashion and should not look for any measure of reform from men until their own sex was emancipated. No one would have dared to speak so illogically to men. Think of telling half-a-dozen men to go home and reform all mankind!... women have constantly to listen to such unjust and unreasonable criticism.[14]*

Women were becoming more experienced at spotting the common ways of attempting to pacify, distract or negate them. As McClung said, "women no longer can be flattered or threatened into silence." We can see such maneuvers in the Persons Case, but we can also see the women's increasingly sharp ability to recognize them and avoid the traps. Of this perception, McClung wrote:

> *For long years the old iniquitous lie has been told us that the hand that rocks the cradle rules the world, but it is no longer believed by thinking women. It is intended more as a bouquet than as a straight statement of facts. It is given as a sedative to soothe us if we grow restless. When driving with a small child we often let the little fellow hold the end of the reins, and if the child really believes he is driving we consider the game successful, but we cannot deceive the average*

Nellie McClung (right) with Prime Minister William Lyon Mackenzie King at a ceremony honoring the five women of the Persons Case.

child very long. So, too, the average woman refuses to be deceived when she is praised like an angel and treated like an idiot.[15]

The activist women were able to find allies. It's surprising how much support prairie women did receive from some men. The support was often rather patronizing in its tone, but it was still more helpful than opposition! Catherine Cleverdon has written that Judge J. Boyd McBride attributed the relative ease with which Albertan women won political recognition to "public appreciation of their heroic pioneering qualities." Many of the women who migrated to Alberta were "by early environment, by university education, and because of interest in public affairs... quite as fitted as men to take their part in the intellectual and administrative development of the new country."

On a more cynical level, one might note that women have also been "allowed" to contribute more to the public scene or the industrial arena whenever their energy has been desperately needed: for frontier development, in times of industrial revolution, or during war years.

Nevertheless, these women persisted with their cause in spite of obstacles, articulated their perceptions of injustice and refused to be silenced, and accepted support where they could find it. As a result of their efforts, history was changed and Canadian women had new support for their rights.

This was the political climate in which Nellie McClung worked, and which she helped to create. McClung did not see herself as a solitary crusader; rather she saw herself as part of something larger. In 1945, looking back on her own life, she wrote:

In Canada we are developing a pattern of life and I know something about one block of that pattern. I know it for I helped to make it, and I can say that now without any pretense of modesty, or danger of arrogance, for I know that we who make the patterns are not important, but the pattern is.[16]

It is important to keep that in mind as we focus on her contribution.

Chapter 8
Keeping Company with Nellie McClung

Jane Brown-John, one of Nellie McClung's grandchildren, remembers an afternoon that she spent at her grandmother's home. Jane was a youngster at the time. She and another young cousin were visiting her grandparents' home in Victoria. Nellie McClung was, by this time, quite frail, but she was still entertaining a wide group of people who would arrive at her home, expected or not, and ask to talk with her. Apparently Sundays were always especially busy. Both Wes and Nellie McClung were apt to invite people home with them after the church service to join them for dinner.

Other days of the week might also see any number of people walking down the lane to their house. Jane remembers that no guest was ever received without an accompanying invitation to tea. On this occasion that Jane recalls, Nellie and Jane's mother, Florence, had been hosting a steady stream of callers all day. Finally, there was absolutely nothing left in the way of refreshments.

A rare and desperate decision was made. The little cousins were told to play very quietly, curtains were drawn, and the house generally made to look empty. Jane says that such measures were so unusual that she has always remembered that afternoon.

Hospitality in the McClung household was generous and almost never ending. Quite literally, many people "kept company" with Nellie McClung and, whenever possible, she relished the opportunity to hear and exchange opinions. Those opinions did not have to agree with her own. She liked the chance to discuss matters directly.

FACING UNFAIRNESS

Throughout her many years of public life, McClung had grown used to hearing comments about herself. As she said herself, people who express their opinions in print or from the platform must expect criticism. Nevertheless, she could still be provoked by comments that she thought were unfair – and that included any attacks on her children. In her second autobiography, she recounted at some length an incident which occurred in 1914 when she was in the midst of the Manitoba suffrage campaign.

She was traveling by train and fell asleep, curled up in her seat on that warm June day. When she wakened she heard her name mentioned and realized that she was the subject under discussion by some people just behind and across the aisle from her. A man was holding forth to several women. They were from the east, he said, and didn't know McClung as well as did the people in Manitoba. "Nellie McClung is nothing but a joke here," he boomed, "and I can tell you that the Government is not worrying about her or her meetings. T.C. Norris is the fellow who should worry. He is the leader of the Opposition, and believe me his candidates lose votes every time she speaks."[1]

The opinionated gentleman waxed on. Nellie McClung was a big woman, he said, badly dressed, with a high-pitched and strident voice, rough and tumble, with big hands and feet. She had a whole raft of children, seven or eight, that she just left to run wild. All the policemen knew them, he declared. Why, his own sister lived near her and she often took the poor kids in to feed and wash them. McClung's husband was a decent sort, apparently, and it was no surprise that he was getting a divorce.

The two "eastern" women did not seem impressed by the narration of shortcomings. From their comments, McClung was sure that they would recognize her if she turned around. Determined not to let the man get away with his comments about her children even though she was prepared to let the rest go, she nonetheless decided not to embarrass him before the women. She waited until the women had left before turning to face her critic. Then she recognized him. He was one of the civil servants from the Public Works Department, she recounted later, a "party healer," and someone who knew her.

All the steam went out of her erstwhile opponent. With a pale face and sweating brow the man confessed to making up his stories. His main concern was whether Nellie McClung would recount the incident in her speeches! He was a pathetic sight and McClung promised that she would not repeat the exchange until, perhaps, some day when she wrote her memoirs. He was like a smear on the window, she said, and so she would just brush him off.

PUBLIC PERCEPTIONS

Naturally enough, Nellie McClung was not universally popular with her contemporaries. Some were delighted to "keep company" with her; others were not. Many of the articles and reviews written about her during her lifetime expressed opinions about her. The majority of the articles were written either for "women's magazines" or for the most general of readerships. The bias of the writers was usually quite transparent. The following excerpt from a 1935 article in a Toronto newspaper gives us an example:

> *Nobody living in Manitoba 20 years ago will ever accept the current fallacy about Nellie McClung that she is wishy-washy; for in bringing the Roblin Government to destruction, she showed more pluck than any man in the province and equal intelligence. Of the filthy abuse poured on her, all fortunately is forgotten, leaving only the derisive tag, Salvation Nell, to carry abroad the suggestion of a virago, which is as false a notion of the author of "Sowing Seeds in Danny" as that she is too sweet. The truth is that she has a lively mind, strong character, and a keen sense of humor.[2]*

Writers delighted in tagging her with titles descriptive of their viewpoints. She was called "Windy Nellie," a "Lady Terror," a "Joan of the West," and "Calamity Nell." She was hailed as a prophet and caricatured as a pestering mosquito. An article in the Ontario Women's Christian Temperance Union paper *The Canadian White Ribbon Tidings* of July 1916 carried the heading: "Nellie McClung of the West: Writer, Lecturer, Cake Baker, Politician, Methodist, Mother." That summed up one reality nicely: Nellie McClung was a complex and multi-talented worker who engaged a wide spectrum of issues.

In the articles written about McClung by her contemporaries, there was often an air of delight and surprise that this politically active woman was also an acceptably competent domestic woman. The article mentioned above from the W.C.T.U. paper began, "Nellie McClung is the kind of personality you can't miss. Drop her into a Canadian Club, a Press Club, a political meeting or her own Methodist Church, and things begin to fizz." The author, Natalie Symmes, did acknowledge that there were mixed reactions to McClung: "Most people like her. Some people don't. But everybody has to have an opinion of some sort, for she's as vivid as a tiger lily at a funeral."

The article reads as if it was quite deliberately reassuring its audience that McClung need not be feared as a radical. Symmes wrote with approval about the "wonderful children" McClung had at home: "Two of them are married, and there's a baby yet, thank heaven, and really if that's the sort of cherub a suffragette has to show – well, there's more to be said in favor of the vote than you'd suppose." After detailing some of McClung's contribution to suffrage efforts, the review ended: "Now she's back home with the babies. That's where she has wanted to

be all along, she says. She'd a heap sight sooner make a cake than a vote. But can she stick? Here's wondering!"[3]

A clipping from an Edmonton newspaper in 1938 does show a rather different sort of reflection. McClung had, apparently, made a number of speeches and addresses in the city about the need for a "God-controlled" world, and a columnist endeavored to push some of her statements to what he thought would be their logical outcome. He asked what would happen to sweatshops and economic inequality in the world she described.

We do not have a copy of her speech to consult. (She often spoke from very brief notes jotted down on the back of old envelopes.) It is difficult to guess its content but one can suppose from other examples that McClung probably suggested some very practical applications of her ideas. It is obvious from the column, however, that her idea of the consequences of her vision were too liberal, and "Liberal," for this columnist. He wrote:

> *I wonder too, if the sign of prosperity in that kind of a Canada would be the size of the dividend cheques paid to the owners of the people's means of life. And the*

liberal party, to which Mrs. McClung for some reason I can never understand,
clings – what sort of an organization would it be if it had the kind of control she
desires? Would it make a difference in armament contracts, and power deals? I
have an idea that the sort of control Mrs. McClung is praying for is that which
would result in a social revolution in the nation.[4]

His "idea" was just about right!

The unabashedly partisan and intimate comments of McClung's friend
Emily Murphy in a 1921 article gives another glimpse of the controversy
which often surrounded McClung. It is apparent that Murphy had her
own inside knowledge of the costs of such controversies, too. She wrote:

...in the clash of conflict, Nellie McClung has had to endure the unfriendly
criticism that comes to all leaders and you may have noticed that epithets and
brick-bats are seldom padded. This has been the history of all women who have
assumed leadership, or broken new trails. The laurel wreath and marble bust
are the gift of later generations who enjoy the happiness for which the leaders
strove.

A modern philosopher has said, "To be famous is to be hated by people who
do not know you," a dictum eminently applicable to the subject of this sketch.
Those most severely critical of Mrs. McClung are strangers to her or who for
some reason or other, fear her influence. In her personality there is a geniality
and open frankness that almost invariably disarm your hostility and which win
you to her cause.[5]

RETELLING THE STORIES

In the years since McClung's death, there have been other general articles on her contribution in Canada. Some have been occasioned by anni-
versaries of particular actions, notably, the successful conclusion of the
Persons Case and the decision to ordain women in the United Church of
Canada. Much of it has focused on simply repeating history's stories. Of
course, this task itself has importance when the history of women is largely
unrecorded and invisible. How could any analytical review, without bio-
graphical detail, be of much help to an audience who knows nothing of
the story?

Candace Savage's book, *Our Nell*, which she subtitled a "scrapbook
biography," provided a helpful and informative survey of material written
by and about McClung. In her preface, Savage declared that she wished
to combine "the immediacy of Nellie's own writings with the detachment
of more distant observers."[6] Savage admitted elsewhere that the book was
intended to be a presentation of McClung, not an academic critique. She
has also said that any particular reflection on McClung's faith perspective

or theology was not her concern.[7]

Until recently there has been little in-depth work done on the suffrage movement or suffragists in Canada – a period of our history in which Nellie McClung was so deeply involved. Catherine Cleverdon's *The Woman's Suffrage Movement in Canada* and Carol Lee Bacchi's *Liberation Deferred?* are two notable exceptions. There is still need for even simple recounting of important events. Few general readers of Canadian history would ever be aware of the issues now often designated as "women's studies" material. The history of women in Canada and their contributions is still largely unwritten.

RENEWED INTEREST

Veronica Strong-Boag's introduction to a new edition of McClung's *In Times Like These*, and of course, the decision of the University of Toronto Press to publish the reprint, was the first real indication of a renewed or reborn interest in Nellie McClung. The essay Strong-Boag provided for the reissue brought a helpfully critical light to bear on the material. It discussed this book in the context of its history and other contemporary events. Because this republication was a sign of revived interest in McClung, I think it is important to take a look at it. As we reflect on our own understanding of McClung, it is helpful to consider the way others have viewed her. Whether we realize it or not, those earlier opinions have probably colored our own.

Published in 1972, the introductory essay in the reissued *In Times Like These* reflects Strong-Boag's own bias at that time against feminism and history. An article written five years later shows some changes in her perspective. (It should be noted that the last 20 years have seen many changes in the consideration of women in history and a growing feminist analysis has added new dimensions to critical reviews.)

Strong-Boag's work provides us with a good illustration of the way history is often interpreted. Those of us who read history tend to forget the effect of the author's perspective. If a historian does not think that the work of, for example, women or native Canadians has been "important," then his or her version of history will reflect that opinion. Similarly, history is also affected by the perspective of the recipient. If we try to interpret past events only in the light of our current experience, we will be adding our own changes.

The most helpful interpreting is possible when the context for the original events and their subsequent renderings is understood. In this case, how can we understand Nellie McClung if we don't know anything about her time?

PROBLEMS OF INTERPRETATION

Let me give you some examples of the effect that interpretation has, using Veronica Strong-Boag's essays as a basis.

Veronica Strong-Boag believed that the mothering ideal was central to McClung's feminism. One cannot deny that concept's contribution, but Strong-Boag's version does not take into account McClung's obvious awareness that the marriage and family experience which provided such strong support for her held very different realities for others. McClung did exalt the *potential* of marriage and motherhood but she was well aware of unenviable experiences of both.

Saying that McClung "never really came to terms with women whose major function would not be motherhood,"[8] as Strong-Boag did, distorts McClung's context. McClung often directed her comments to married women for two reasons. First, they formed the largest part of her audience. Second, she knew how difficult it could be for women with children to define new roles for themselves. Their home situation did not give them much freedom to experiment with new roles! Nevertheless, McClung argued that she and other women could be all anyone wanted as mothers and wives and still engage in a wider frontier. Although some of her suggestions would have best suited women with economic freedom, she did think that there was a variety of ways in which others could help with child rearing.

McClung's arguments that marriage should be a "divine partnership based on mutual love and community of interest" (in *In Times Like These*) presented a model quite different from the servant role usually assigned to wives in her time. She bore out her ideas in work for laws which would support such a partnership model. For example, McClung took the opportunity she had as a member of the Legislative Assembly in Alberta to argue for a variety of bills which attempted to revise laws on behalf of women. These included pension revisions and changes to the dower act and the minimum wage act.

In much the same way, Strong-Boag claimed that McClung's demand for women's rights was presented as a "logical extension of traditional views of female moral superiority and maternal responsibility."[9] That, however, does not take into consideration McClung's strongly biblical sense of justice and the theological problem of injustice with which she continued to wrestle.

Similarly, Strong-Boag's summary of McClung's picture of a redeemed

Canada has its gaps. Strong-Boag wrote: "It was missionary; it was rural; it was assimilative; and it was dry." She misses the point that a redeemed Canada would also have been, in McClung's opinion, just toward women.

Strong-Boag repeatedly read moralism as the motive for McClung's actions, rather than feminism and a passion for justice. This can be seen in her discussion of McClung's work for prohibition. Strong-Boag's comments on the prohibitionists are reminiscent of caricatures of their work, and of present-day ridicule and contempt for what is seen as narrow-mindedness. Damning them with faint praise, she wrote that the "temperance people were more than the cranks we now consider them"!

The feminist prohibitionists were not narrow-minded prudes. Instead, they contended that women and children suffered directly from alcohol abuses, and that the whole system of liquor promotion was aimed at exploiting people. Perhaps it was Strong-Boag's own bias which cued Kildare Dobbs's derogatory opinion of McClung in his review of the reissued book; perhaps they already shared the same perspective. Cloaking his comments in a factual veil, Dobbs's derision is still clearly visible: "A middle class WASP to her unbending backbone, she (McClung), was not only feminist but prohibitionist."[10] It is hard to tell which was the greater offense in Dobbs's opinion!

Strong-Boag's anti-feminist bias at the time of her writing was made quite evident at the close of her Introduction. In a paragraph very reminiscent of opponents to the modern women's movement, she levelled a charge of "man-hating" at McClung.

> *There was another strain on the practicality of her position. Despite her close social and political relationships with a number of men, McClung's arguments often have anti-masculine overtones. Men were frequently portrayed as aggressive, selfish, and uncontrollable. Women were their victims. This myopia is often an unfortunate corollary to the claim of female moral superiority. It leads to a type of reverse sexual discrimination that is one of the most serious flaws in the feminist argument.[11]*

Can you imagine McClung's response? She would probably have snapped back that women were not just often *portrayed* as victims, they often *were* victims.

Another comment, made almost in passing as an act of absolution, strikes the ears of current-day feminists as equally strange. With an air of generosity this time, Strong-Boag declared: "the failure of feminism was not in McClung's particular shortcomings, but in her successors' failure to reappraise the situation and avoid the same pitfalls." We might say that that sounds like a funeral eulogy for an arguably empty coffin.

THE ECONOMIC CONTEXT

More light is shed on Strong-Boag's view of the decline of feminist activism in her 1977 article "Canadian Feminism of the 1920s: The Case of Nellie L. McClung." There she cited an increase in the emphasis on homelife in the postwar years: "The terror of battle and regimentation of the military had left many men desperately in need of domestic solace." [12] One might add, "not to mention jobs!"

Strong-Boag quoted a variety of calls to women for a return to the home, without, apparently, any awareness of the pressures being brought to bear by a postwar and patriarchal economy. She declared that the growing disillusionment about the notion of women's moral superiority had undermined maternalism as a justification and explanation for public service, and had left the women directionless. "Sacrifice, maternal and otherwise, had not changed the world very much. Old prejudices against women in education and employment were among the many discouraging signs." In contrast to Strong-Boag's assessment, I would argue that the prejudices were contributing causes, not signs.

To read that period of Canadian history without attention to economic pressures leaves us vulnerable to a very liberal and deceptive version. Tiredness and disillusionment may well have lowered women's resistance, but there were also strong economic forces at work. "Even her own quotes might have raised Strong-Boag's suspicion. She wrote that in the early '20s an observer of the University of Toronto – which was at least technically a coeducational institution – declared: "Practically, there seems to be a strong cross-current of prejudice which prevents free intercourse between men and women students." Nor, she noted, were universities "the only offenders. The phrase 'Girls No Longer Wanted' (the title of an article in the *Canadian Home Journal* of March 1922) seemed to keynote the postwar years." [14] "Girls" were no longer wanted so "girls" were being sent home. The pressure was on for women to conveniently disappear into domesticity.

I have considered Veronica Strong-Boag's comments at some length, to show that modern views of Nellie McClung may not be any less diverse than those held while she was living. Strong-Boag's contribution still stands as a well-respected portion of the fledgling body of material on McClung. Any subsequent commentator can expect to be challenged by Strong-Boag's framework and conclusions. Even if we come to different conclusions, we should have some idea of the alternative opinions.

Our own assessment of McClung is, after all, dependent on our own values and our own perspectives. Whether or not we find companionship with Nellie McClung in our own generation depends on who she was, and on who we are. It depends on whether or not we feel she has anything to say to our own experience. Of course, to decide this, we have to be able to identify our own experience!

Women who search for a nurturing and sustaining community are beginning to discover that they can receive companionship both from contemporaries and from a rediscovery – or perhaps a discovery! – of foremothers who confronted many of the same dynamics of oppression in similar and different issues. Nellie L. McClung can be one such companion. When we become familiar with her contribution to our history, we discover many attitudes and experiences which have their parallel in current situations. The strongest sense of companionship will probably be felt by those who share her love for the church even while being frustrated by its immobility on certain issues.

TENSIONS IN MINISTRY

Let me explain from my own situation. My training and vocation is that of an ordained minister in the United Church of Canada. In the years that I have spent in parish ministry, I have become increasingly aware of an ongoing struggle to decide just how important pastoral care and prophetic challenge are in our ministries.

Is one more important than the other? We hear mixed messages from parishioners. Some express disappointment at the lack of strong direction coming from the pulpit. They feel that their minister should be helping them with the hard choices that confront them. Others are dissatisfied because they feel that sermons dwell too much on hard words of challenge and do not provide a warm and nurturing environment for comfort and healing.

As ministers, many of us struggle to know how to speak faithfully to the scripture readings and still keep these concerns in mind. If we know that someone is upset or angered by a sermon on Sunday, how do we keep a relationship which will let us minister to their pastoral needs if a relative dies on Wednesday?

One of the joys of parish ministry is that we are permitted a rare intimacy with the members of our congregations. We are often brought into the center of some of the most significant times in people's lives. That can be one of the great gifts of this vocation, but it presents its own problems too. When is it appropriate to murmur words of condolence and offer warmly supportive listening? When is it more faithful to express challenge, disagreement, or disapproval? When love for the people and love for the Word produce difficult dilemmas, what is to be done with the tension that is created?

Women ministers often encounter an added dilemma. As women, we can find ourselves in the strange position of having to try to explain – without alienating a group to whom we are also called to provide pastoral care – why women should be understood to have worth equal to men, or why laws and language must reflect that equality and awareness. Feminist women ministers may feel the strangeness most keenly. Our perception of society and theological position makes sexism as offensive as racism, yet we endure countless discussions which contend that discrimination does not even exist! In such situations, I have often felt torn between frustration at what seems to be selective blindness, and some satisfaction that at least the discussions are happening!

Sometimes such debates arise over particular issues. One current example is the growing movement to abolish exclusive images and phrases in our churches. Feminist women have declared that they do not hear themselves named when "sons of God" and the "brotherhood of all mankind" are welcomed into the "Father's house" of salvation. Change, however, does not come quickly or easily. Those responsible for leadership in public worship – including women – are trapped by the reality of existing supplies, often carefully and painstakingly purchased with meager funds, of hymn books and worship aids which may be rampantly sexist and almost totally unusable from the standpoint of feminist awareness. To add another complexity, tradition has often held that such resources are donated "in memoriam." There is, therefore, a deep emotional attachment to such material. How, with integrity intact, shall a worship leader resolve such a dilemma?

There are, of course, many other examples of the tension between pastoral care and prophetic leadership. In a time of dramatically increasing domestic violence, for instance, few ministers can remain immune to involvements with, and concerns for, abused women and children. Knowing that deeply ingrained perceptions usually entrap the victims, how will pastors deal with their own understanding of justice and their feelings of anger as they endeavor to call the abused into freedom? Women who believe that their husbands have the right to "discipline" them, and that they only receive abuse because they have somehow "earned" it, are very slow even to identify the abuse, let alone to press charges. Economic dependence also limits the options for many women. With the urgency of an individual's needs threatening to overwhelm her, how can she confront the broad social evils which are producing the problem?

Even these brief illustrations should indicate some of the tensions between pastoral and prophetic ministry. How, then, does one deal with the dilemma? Again, for the moment, let me focus on the alternatives for women like me.

Resolving the Dilemmas

One possibility, of course, is a decision to forcibly resolve the dilemma by denying one element of ministry. This has, naturally, major consequences. No matter which element one drops from one's ministry, it will occasion some unrest from at least part of the constituency, but most parishioners would probably object more strongly to the absence of nurturing care than to the loss of challenge.

One can also choose to leave the problem – and the ministry – behind, by an exodus from a confining land. In this instance, that would mean leaving the Christian church as most of us know it. This has been the route that the radical feminist Mary Daly has suggested. In 1971, she invited the congregation at Harvard Memorial Church to follow her then and there into exodus.[15] The image has been discussed widely since. Although we may understand the frustration which leads to such a call, such a solution does nothing to change the root problem. Exodus is for those who see no hope in remaining.

Personally, I certainly do not think that these dilemmas will be quickly resolved, but I still hope for transforming change within the church. I do believe that we have to find ways to renew our courage and commitment while living *within* this difficult reality. I think we can do that if we are nurtured by a sense of community with others who have experienced the same cost of discipleship. And that community includes Nellie L. McClung.

(I realize that I have been speaking specifically out of my own experience as an ordained woman. However, I do not believe that the tension and dilemmas that I have described belong exclusively to women in ordered ministries. I hear very similar experiences from women who exercise their ministries in other ways. Many men might also identify their own version of this pastoral/prophetic dilemma. I have begun, however, with my own experience.)

A COMPANION ON THE WAY

I believe that Nellie McClung understood what it felt like to be pulled between a wish to lovingly embrace people and the need she felt to sometimes challenge them. In her case, the tension was not caused by employment within the church but by her active lay participation in ministry and by the Christian faith which was the ground of her being and action. For women in the church today, it can be helpful to look at the way in which McClung did her work. She endeavored to close any gaps between herself and those whom she wished to reach. She made it difficult for people to distance her as an "other." When she could not be

Wes and Nellie celebrating a wedding anniversary.

"written off" in that way, it was difficult to either silence or ignore her, and that gave McClung her audience. She knew very well that a listening audience was vulnerable to new ideas and possible conversion.

Although she did not have the same forms of pastoral/prophetic tension that I may have, she experienced her own versions of that same tension. She struggled to find ways to challenge the church's stand on one issue or another without becoming destructive of its unity. On both secular or religious issues, McClung's strong opinions often brought disagreement. Like many others, she had the delicate task of maintaining relationships with people who might be allies on one issue and opponents on another.

Transparent affection for people in general and a humorous appreciation for life's inanities lent an endearing warmth to McClung's critical appraisals. Some of her most strident opponents admitted admiration for the persistence and success of her efforts. The passion of her convictions provided the energy required to keep actions going even when the cost was high.

She was also careful to maintain relationships which nurtured and sustained her. She always asserted that her husband's love and support was critical to her endeavors. And she had a wide network of friends and colleagues with whom she shared a sense of community. It is obvious, from her papers, that McClung maintained an extensive correspondence, often writing, and receiving, letters of support, interest, and concern – as well as those with a more businesslike intent.

When we identify common denominators between McClung's experience and our own, we open the possibility that we can learn from her. Perhaps we can find fresh strength and encouragement by keeping company with her.

Wes and Nellie's 50th wedding anniversary celebration in 1946.

CHAPTER 9

THE NOT-SO-SMALL LEGACY OF NELLIE L. MCCLUNG

Nellie McClung published the second volume of her autobiography in 1945. In its introduction she wrote that she would have liked to title it "Without Regret." She was in the mood to celebrate the richness of her life. On the other hand, she was keenly aware of things she had not done. After ten years of steadily failing health she had come very close to dying in 1943. That crisis brought new insight, she declared.

> As my brain cleared, I had a great longing to live. There was good mileage in me yet, and there were so many things that I wanted to do and had always been so sure that I would do... I would have worked harder if I had have known that life could be so soon over. I always knew that our spiritual forces were not keeping pace with our mechanical development... What a time to be alive! And what a poor time to die. So I lived... But still I cannot look back without regret. I can see too many places where I could have been more obedient to the heavenly vision, for a vision I surely had for the creation of a better world.
>
> But I hope I am leaving at least some small legacy of truth.[1]

We are beginning to understand the nature of that legacy.

Several years ago I was asked to speak to a dozen churchwomen at a senior citizens' residence in Saskatoon. As I was in the midst of my research and reflection on Nellie McClung, I decided to make her the focus of our discussion. I was delighted to discover that in the group of 12 women, most had heard of McClung and many had stories of their own to tell about her. Several had heard her speak. Others had heard their parents speak about her.

That evening reminded me once again that Nellie McClung is part of our recent past. Whether or not a great deal of formal history has been written about her, there is a strong oral history still available. Some of the most senior women in our midst still remember the historical situation

One of many portraits that appeared in newspapers.

which McClung confronted. They know her "relevance" from personal experience.

PERCEPTUAL PREJUDICES

Younger women have recently begun to look and listen for the stories of their past which will give them a greater understanding of their present. It is probably more difficult for these later generations to get an integrated picture of Nellie McClung. Separated from her presence by time, we may pick up those elements of her life and work which most appeal to us, and ignore, deliberately or unwittingly, other components which seem less meaningful or more foreign.

Such selective perception operates, however, even in the presence of the real person or situation. Nellie McClung was seldom seen as an integrated eclectic in her own time. Her own generation might well have preferred to focus on her work as a "good, Christian woman" and to downplay her feminism. Those in our present generation who are most interested in her might well be more attracted to her feminism than her faith. Such preferences reflect the observers, more than they do the real Nellie McClung.

What happens if we overlook both her faith and her feminism? Well, we are left only with an impression that McClung was a "character" – an entertaining, colorful, but insignificant player on history's stage. Ironically, this is as effective a way as any to trivialize a person's contribution. "Characters" can be quotable and even, for a time, popular, but they are seen as no more relevant to our own living than an amiable and eccentric relative.

Nellie McClung was a Christian feminist woman who, while remaining deeply committed to her family and her church, wrote, lobbied, spoke, preached, and marched. She was witty and eminently quotable – in fact, her style seemed designed for easy and memorable quotations. If she was extraordinary it was because she used her talents so thoroughly. Women who wish to emulate her do not need to copy her talents, but rather need to use their own just as thoroughly.

It is not surprising that a wide variety of people have celebrated McClung. Her diverse gifts attracted a very mixed audience. Nevertheless, I believe, it is only when she is understood as a Christian feminist woman that a deep companionship with her is possible. Christian feminist women in this day and age who are also committed to persistent involvement in the church will find

A family Christmas card.

McClung relevant in a way that secular or nonfeminist critics cannot.

For example, in a Master's thesis entitled "Small Legacy of Truth," Patricia Louise Verkruysse studied McClung's novels and came to the conclusion that McClung's contribution to Canadian literature was not as important, ultimately, as her "political feminist achievements." At the end of her work she applied some advice, once given by Virginia Woolf to the critic of contemporary literature, to the attitude McClung had about her own "small legacy":

> Let them take a wider, a less personal view of modern literature, and look indeed upon the writers as if they were engaged upon some vast building, which being built by common effort, the separate workman may well remain anonymous.[2]

That perception notwithstanding, Verkruysse's view of McClung is that when she died, "many of her concepts and prescriptions were already either archaic or irrelevant" and that McClung failed to recognize society's growing rejection of the old values upon which her vision for "the creation of a better world had been founded."[3]

Similarly, Veronica Strong-Boag wrote, in her introduction to the re-issue of *In Times Like These*, that,

> She failed, as did the majority of American feminists, to provide modern women with satisfactory identity models. Instead, in a newly secular world and an increasingly permissive society, she left women with a missionary role which emphasized the centrality of the maternal experience. McClung's rural sympathies made her analysis appear ever more irrelevant in an urban age.[4]

This assessment is predicated on inherent biases, and it takes a little unraveling to sort out the tangle of presuppositions. Lumping McClung with "the majority of American feminists" is unhelpful and inappropriate. Others have argued that McClung demonstrated a particularly Canadian brand of feminism.[5] Since McClung's activism was provoked by economic, political, religious and regional issues particular to Canada, I think that they make the stronger case.

Strong-Boag dismissed McClung's "rural sympathies" with what could be called urban arrogance. Many parts of Canada are still grounded in a rural economy.

Finally, Strong-Boag misses the point – McClung was trying to encourage women to adopt a missionary role. She would have seen that vocation as particularly important in a "newly secular world and an increasingly permissive society."

A FEMINIST EVANGELIST

Nellie McClung was an evangelist. Much of the power and energy of her public work came from her conviction that she truly had Good News for the people. Remember when she declared that she hoped that her art had not obscured her sermons? McClung was a preacher, and the fact that she was so well heard means that she was a *good* preacher. Her son Mark says that he is sure that, had she been a man, she would have been another John Wesley!

She preached liberation for women because that was consistent with the gospel. She preached a new, "fair deal" for everyone. "Evangelist" is not a word with universally acceptable connotations, but it really describes her. She believed that women, out of their own experience, have a unique and positive missionary role.

In 1919 McClung declared, "There may be a new religion preached from our pulpits when there are as many women preachers as men. There may be a new interpretation of scripture. It is quite likely there may be a new type of hero, and a new conception of heroism and courage, and of success..."[6] Was that not a prophecy of a new feminist theology?

On another occasion she wrote, "If we had more women leaders, preachers, and editorial writers, we would have more of the spindle and less of the spear in our mentality."[7] In the same piece she also wrote, "... I believe women in public life could help the cause of peace by their ability to compromise. They can step down more easily than men, swallow their pride and eat humble pie. They have had to do it in this manmade world where humility has never been regarded as a manly virtue." In theological terms, we might say that she was seeing a transformation of a quality of *slavery* into a gift of Christian *servanthood*.

DO NOT FAIL TO HEAR

Mrs. Nellie L. McClung

LECTURE

On Woman Suffrage, Temperance Issues and Things Political.

AN OPEN DISCUSSION IS DESIRED

Mrs. McClung is acknowledged to be one of the foremost platform speakers in the west to-day.

THE TOWN HALL, KILLARNEY

THURSDAY, JUNE THE 18TH

AT EIGHT O'CLOCK SHARP

Reserved Seats 35c.   General Admission 25c.

Plan of Hall at Evans' Drug Store.

A typical poster used by McClung supporters.

Feminism in Canada has, like feminism elsewhere, evolved into something different from the feminism of McClung and her colleagues. If that earlier feminism was part of a first stage, then the feminism of modern women is of a second or later stage.

Some of the preliminary battles have been won, it can be argued. McClung's agitation for basic recognition of women as having rights is no longer necessary. Indeed, people from diametrically opposite camps could argue that McClung's feminism is now outdated. Some feminists now would find McClung's reform methodology too limiting and her religious fervor quaint but naive. Other nonfeminist women would declare that women already have total equality – at least as much equality as any real woman wants – making McClung's arguments unnecessary.

But most people live somewhere between these two viewpoints. Feminist pastors, fresh from universities and lively debates between the two polarities, move to pastoral charges and discover that most of their parishioners have neither caught up with modern feminism, nor accorded women complete equality. Instead of seeming outdated, McClung's missionary fervor looks highly appropriate!

In spite of the rights finally recognized in this century, the vast majority of the congregations with whom those pastors work may well have no knowledge of previous struggles or any perceptions of the present-day battles. Even those who identify past injustices around, for example, property rights or suffrage, seldom make connections between those issues and the new faces which oppression dons: inadequate or nonexistent pensions for women, lack of daycare facilities, increasing cutbacks on social programs, increasing pressure on women to leave the workplace, lack of financial recognition for homemakers... The list is just a beginning.

It could be claimed that the visible feminist movement in Canada exists largely in a ghetto – a comfortable ghetto of upper middle-class, educated women. Such a claim would be based on the perception that most of the high profile leadership comes from this "ghetto." Much less public attention is given to the struggles of lower income, less educated women.

Inroads have been made on male preserves, if a few high paying, high profile positions are counted. But there is still little public support for changes affecting the majority of working-class women. The mass media focus attention on the few women in upper management positions or the women who are ministers of legislatures or parliaments. Besides the fact that these women are part of a small minority, we may find that their individual "successes" have little impact on the lives of the rest of women.

It could even be argued that feminist energy has been largely marginalized into a small elite. Ironically, this elite is cited as proof that things have really changed for women when, in reality, their marginalizing may be yet another tool of oppression. As long as there is at least one token woman, a company or a government can use her presence as "proof" that it is not discriminatory!

THE NEW FACES OF OPPRESSION

The majority of women in our society and in our congregations have the same lack of clarity about the oppression of women as our grandmothers had. Haven't we tended to accept the changes that have come, with little or no thought, and perhaps small gratitude? Haven't we generally ignored this generation's reenactment of the same forces of oppression?

Women are still being treated as exceptional when they do competent work; women still receive blame as a group when one woman "fails." McClung identified her fear of this when she first contemplated the possibility of a Cabinet position. She reflected:

> *I knew I could make a good speech. I knew I could persuade people, and I knew*
> *I had a real hold on the people of Manitoba, especially the women, but I also*

knew that the whole situation was fraught with danger, for if I as the first woman to hold a Cabinet position failed, it would be a blow to women everywhere. I could easily undo all I had done for I knew the world would be critical of women for a long time. If a woman succeeded, her success would belong to her as an individual. People would say she was an exceptional woman. She had a "masculine" mind. Her success belonged to her alone, but if she failed, she failed for all women everywhere.[8]

Women still face much the same attitude today. Certainly, women ministers still experience this reality, all too easily becoming known as "exceptional women" or, conversely, suffering because of some other female minister's history. Parishes talk of "having had a woman minister once" and since it didn't "work out," they want to stick to men from now on. The fact that such parishes have also had unhappy relationships with male clergy doesn't seem to have any significance!

The trick of labeling women "exceptional" is, of course, particularly seductive – it is easy to overlook the inherent condescension. If a woman is competent, she must be exceptional.

We also need to acknowledge that women in Canada are not a homogenized whole. Women in nonurban Canada might well be puzzled by Strong-Boag's declaration of an "urban age." Their experience often sounds different from that of their urban sisters.

When supportive resources diminish, they are withdrawn first from low population areas. Women in need in nonurban centers find few local support services. The logic of low funding puts whatever services there are in more densely populated regions.

Women in urban settings, on the other hand, experience higher costs of living and inadequate services for their crowded community. Broad generalizations and oversimplifications contribute to oppression. We don't pay enough careful attention to the *different* situations that women face.

That inadequate services are "justified" with talk of "restraint" does not obscure the consequences, either. "Restraint" and "recession" are also cited as justifications for dumping women back into "The Home"! For those who think that this is a new phenomenon it can be rather startling to read McClung's words to women after the First World War. Women had left their homes to serve their country, but once the men returned from war the question, McClung said, was: "Will women go back?"

The bars are down, the bombs of war have blown them to atoms, the walls of prejudice have been crumbled by the shells of necessity. But let no one think that human nature has been regenerated and that the prejudice against women has completely died away... You were not employed because you were wanted, ladies, but because you were needed, *and there was nobody else! They are hoping that you will go back to your home and split your time into a hundred odds and ends of occupations, cooking a little, sewing a little, washing, ironing, financing, teaching, social work...*[9]

McClung urged women to claim the place that had been won. As she said, "It always was ours but we had not taken out our papers." That insight would win appreciation from even the most radical of feminists!

If we look at McClung from the perspective of Christian, feminist churchwomen, we see a companion. I use that word "companion" quite deliberately. At times the words "role model" have come to mind, but that doesn't quite fit. Something that Mary Daly once wrote helped to clarify my sense of uneasiness.[10] She has said that the very idea of "model" was part of a patriarchal mindset which encouraged people first to slavishly imitate a master or father-figure and then to reject this figure in order to be themselves. She suggested that it is significant that the Latin term *modulus* means a "a small measure"!

Women today can be free of this old imitation-rejection syndrome, Daly said. Instead, women can spark courage in each other to affirm their own unique being. McClung would much rather "spark courage," I am sure, than sit on some pedestal as a model. She was always leery of pedestals!

This distinction can also remind us that McClung and her own style cannot be transplanted wholesale into this generation. In confronting some of the realities of oppression (many of which still exist and which still plague women), however, she demonstrated some strategies and techniques from which we can learn. Knowing more about her may well spark some new ideas as well as courage.

A SENSE OF MISSION

Let me say again that, although a wide audience might appreciate these strategies, something important will be missing if the sense of mission is dropped or overlooked. A sense of mission can be a great resource for the ongoing struggle. The challenge of the gospel still lives in tension with love and grace and, difficult as such language can be to secular ears, Christians are still called to live in the "already and not yet" of God's kingdom. Increasingly secular as Canadian society is, the call remains the same. Mission is not something which "has had its day" and can now be abandoned.

Having said that, then, and from within this context of a sense of shared discipleship with McClung, what are the important elements of her legacy?

Shared experience can produce deep bonds and give profound integrity and credibility to a person's words. Nellie McClung was very aware of this. Remember when she told her brother that she had been accepted by women because they knew that she knew what she was talking about? Henry H. Mitchell has shown that Ezekiel was a biblical character who had to learn the same truth. Mitchell quotes from Ezekiel 3:15:

> *Then I came to them of the captivity at Tel-Abib, that dwelt by the river of Chebar, and I sat where they sat, and remained there astonished among them seven days.*

Then he does a powerful retelling of the story.

> *Here was a young man who saw himself in inflated, idealistic terms...*
>
> *As he says in the vision just before our text, he was resisting in the heat of his spirit, and he was compelled of God to become priest-prophet. He was made by God to identify with the needy, hurting people of whom he himself, had he only stopped to think, must have been numbered as one. He did then, not in the*

vision but in the history which unfolded thereafter, what he was supposed to do. He did in fact begin to sit where they sat...

    No person of any group, whether of age, race, social or economic status, or nationality, is exempt from the obligation to sit where those "other" people sit. [11]

Mitchell added: "Prophets though we be, we must be prophets within and not outside of the communities in which we serve."

Mitchell's sermon gives helpful words to understand the source of much of McClung's power. She did not distance herself from the community that she addressed. In contrast, as I've tried to show, she even worked to keep anyone else from distancing her!

IMPLICATIONS FOR TODAY

The implications are clear for feminist churchwomen, but perhaps not easy to hear. Reflection on the realities of parish life, however, quickly reveals the wisdom of this stance. Besides being faithful, it is obviously effective! Most change seems to happen best in the context of relationship. People are more likely to hear the prophetic word when it comes from someone they trust. Compassion breeds in the time spent "sitting together" and that compassion can bring great pastoral insight into why it is so difficult for women to throw over known oppression for unknown freedom, why "security" has such allure or why apathy thrives.

Nellie McClung was no more able to identify with everyone than anyone else can, but she repeatedly and convincingly demonstrated her sense of companionship with those to whom she spoke. It seems likely that it was this sense of intimacy which guided her selection of styles of address. McClung found ways to make herself heard. She adapted the method to suit the opportunity. Therein lies another lesson.

McClung took advantage of the openings available to her to forward her opinions and work for change. In a time when lecture circuits were common and public addresses popular, McClung used those opportunities to do her work. As the nature of communications began to change, McClung was one who urged the churches to be ready to use radio in evangelism. (Mark McClung has said that she couldn't get the United Church to budge on broadcasting and she was "just livid" about it. [12])

Nellie McClung used the opportunities that were available to her to forward her opinions and to work for change. We cannot hope to copy her approach and have it work for all our situations. Humor, for example, depends on its context for laughter. Some of McClung's wry whimsy is still effective today, but much of her most pointed satire was totally involved with specific situations and events. The material could not be successfully transplanted. But the knowledge of humor's usefulness can.

Humor of itself, of course, does not bring about revolution. Reinhold Niebuhr has said, "[laughter's]... efficacy is limited to preserving the self-respect of the slave against the master. It does not extend to the destruction of slavery."[13] Nevertheless McClung might say that a slave who had learned self-respect had already taken the first step away from slavery.

As I've said before, McClung was not a career humorist. Satire was not an end in itself. She used humor only when she deemed it appropriate. Many of us could well identify a similar need to temper our own use of humor with an understanding of our listeners and the situation.

The same discretion must be applied to imitating McClung's particular way with words. Although many of her parables are still effective, it is more to the point to note her use of parable and to develop contemporary versions of that effective teaching tool.

Another element of McClung's style worthy of note was her directness in confronting offensive issues or persons. Whether it was Premier Roblin or the insurance underwriters, she did not overlook the possibility of conversion! When that did not achieve the necessary results then she tried other avenues. For example, when Roblin refused to let her speak to his Cabinet about women's suffrage, he ended one meeting with an invitation to her to return any time. He told her that she amused him. McClung commented later that his voice "dripped fatness." She said she left him with these words:

> I'll not be back, Sir Rodmond, not in your time. I hadn't much hope of doing any good by coming, but I thought it only fair to give you the chance. I'll not be back, but it's just possible that you will hear from me, not directly, but still you'll hear, and you may not like what you hear, either."
>
> "Is this a threat?" he laughed.
>
> "No," I said. "It's a prophecy."[14]

Closely tied to this directness was her persistence. One can, with history's telescope, forget how many years McClung worked for particular changes. Remembering the length of time that her efforts took may offer companionship to weary witnesses today.

Even as we find companionship with McClung, however, we should be reminded by her own life that she never underestimated the importance of being part of a warmly supportive, nurturing community. For her, that included her family, close personal friends, and a wide circle of colleagues and fellow workers. McClung's resilience, she would have been the first to say, had much to do with this constant sense of loving support. Although her name often attracted particular attention, there was nothing of the Lone Ranger in her. She would, most likely, have been in total agreement with Virginia Woolf's statement about the relative unimportance of individual workers. She did, indeed, make that statement about being "part of a pattern" which carried much the same message.

PASSION AND PURPOSE

There is one other element which was central to the way Nellie McClung worked. She always knew why she wanted change. Anger sometimes fueled her vigor but she was never just "blowing steam" in public. She made the following comment in reference to the heady days in 1914 when she was helping to make history, but her words are almost a summary of her creative ministry and vocation:

> We were in deadly earnest and our one desire was to bring about a better world for everyone. We were not men-haters as our opponents loved to picture us... We were not like the angry woman who cleans her house and beats her carpets to work off her rage. Ours was not a rage, it was a passion.[15]

I think that there is great wisdom in understanding the difference between rage and passion. While rage can be immobilizing, passion can spark new action. While rage may serve the achievement of short-term goals, passion enables the long, arduous journey. Rage can empower a strongly confrontational stance when that is required (as in Jesus' overturning of tables in the temple) but passion can deepen the interpersonal relationships necessary to remain *with* the community.

Passion can give life to a new spirit of feminist outreach. In this distinction between rage and passion, women can apprehend a fundamental pattern for their own ministry – and find a renewed commitment to living in that difficult land which lies between challenge and love. If activist women, as McClung speculated, are humanity's last hope for a new world of peace, that mission will need passionate commitment. The legacy she has left is itself one of encouragement and challenge.

> The women are our last reserves. If they cannot heal the world, we are lost, for they are the last we have – we cannot call the angels down... The trumpets are calling for healers and binders who will not be appalled at the task of nursing back to health a wounded world, shot to pieces by injustice, greed, cruelty, and wrong thinking."[16]

Two Short Stories by Nellie L. McClung

Banking in London
& How It Feels to Be a Defeated Candidate

These two stories are reproduced from two collections of short stories, pictured below: *Be Good to Yourself,* and *All We Like Sheep.* Thanks to Thomas Allen and Son, Ltd.

Banking in London

by Nellie L. McClung

I determined to deposit my money. I knew that was an easy thing to do, even pleasant, the simplest form of banking operation; and so with my money in my black bag I entered a bank.

To the young lady behind the wicket I addressed myself. "I wish to open an account," I said. I spoke casually. I wanted her to understand that banking money was a daily experience with me.

"Yes, madam," she said, but not in that eager, welcoming way I had expected; "but you must see the manager."

"Where is he?" I asked, looking around at the many men I saw through the brass lattice, perched up on their high stools.

"You must wait for him in the waiting-room," she said. Her manner was dignified and grave. I gathered from it that a bank manager was not to be achieved at a single bound, but must be won by patient waiting.

Through the blue velvet hangings she directed me to the waiting-room. It was dark, small and empty. I waited. The steady rumble of London's afternoon traffic went by. When my eyes grew accustomed to the gloom I found the heavily shrouded window, and, drawing back the funereal hangings, I gazed into the street. I counted the buses; I figured out my expenses for the day – and I waited.

A door led from the waiting-room. It was marked "Private." I believed it led to the retreat of the manager whom I would see. I watched it hopefully; it might open any moment. Time passed.

Suddenly I looked at my watch: it was after half-past two. The place seemed to be deserted. A fear broke over me – they had locked up and gone home – they had forgotten me! The night watchman would find me, here, with this money! He might shoot me!

I was leaving the waiting-room hurriedly, but to my relief I found no one had gone. The young lady was still in the cage, the occupants of the high stools were still repeating sums of money to each other. Fear making me bold, I again addressed the young lady.

"Tell me," I said, "what is the delay? I see I have begun wrong some way. I am a stranger, you see, and I do not know your ways. Perhaps you do not take money on Mondays; maybe you have all the money you want. Or should I give a three-days notice of motion, or wire ahead for a reservation? I see I am wrong, but please tell me how to go on from here."

She looked at me wonderingly.

"Has it anything to do with Lent," I said, "or full moon, or the Lord Mayor's show?"

"Oh no," she replied, puzzled, "not at all. The manager will see you presently. I will tell him again."

"Yes do," I said; "and please tell him I do not want to borrow money, but to deposit it. I think you could not have made that plain. I know people who want to borrow money have to wait, but not depositors."

"Certainly, madam," she said, politely.

Again I went back to the dim little room, and again time passed. A man came out of the private door, hat in hand, and passed into the street, but still the door turned its inhospitable back on me. The shadows lengthened in the street as the afternoon wore away.

I looked out through the blue hangings to reassure myself that the staff were still at work, and saw one fellow untwisting his legs from around the shank of his stool. It looked to me as if he were getting ready to go.

A sudden impulse seized me. I would see what was behind the closed door. She had said the manager would see me presently. All right. He would if his eyesight happened to be good – he would see me! I knocked.

The door opened, and a tall man in gray stood in the murky doorway.

"Well?" he asked. His tone betokened a certain amount of resignation, not untinged with annoyance.

"Did the girl at the wicket tell you I was here?" I asked, trying to speak haughtily, but finding my courage seeping away. I began to see that it was presumptuous of me to bother the staff with my little personal affairs.

He disdained my question. "Now what is it, exactly, that you want?" he asked.

"I want to open an account," I said, "and I made the mistake of thinking this was a bank. It is marked so, but it must be a mistake."

"Do come in," he said.

I came in.

"Now, do sit down." His tone gave me to understand that my habit of not coming in and not sitting down was very annoying.

I sat down.

He spread his hands on the table as if it were a *seance*.

"Now, tell me what it is," he said patiently.

"I want to open an account," I said doggedly. "I still want to, and it's the same account I wanted to open an hour ago."

"Very good," he said "very good. We are not refusing money, but you must give me a reference."

I began all over again.

"I must be using the wrong words," I said, "you have misunderstood me. But see, I have the money, and I want you to take it and keep it for me. I don't want you to loan me money; I have it here in Bank of England notes."

"Even so," he said, "we must have a reference."

I could think of nothing that would be both suitable and becoming.

"What do you want a reference for?" I asked at last. "Are you collecting references?"

"It is our rule," he said with finality.

I put the money in my bag and stood up.

"Good afternoon," I said. "I'm sorry I have to go. I've had a pleasant time, but it is getting late, and I really must find a bank."

"This is a bank," he said, "and you will have to give a reference wherever you go in England. Don't you know someone in London?"

"Give me time," I said, "I have only been here since Saturday."

"You must know someone," he persisted.

"I do," I replied, "I know Lady Astor."

"Who is she?" he asked wearily. I knew now I was undergoing an intelligence test.

I shook my head. "If you have never heard of the British House of Commons," I said severely, "it's too long a story for me to begin."

"Who else do you know?" he asked. "Some business man perhaps?"

"Yes," I said, "I know Sir Charles Starmer."

There was no gleam of intelligence in the cold eyes that regarded me. I must explain further.

"Sir Charles Starmer," I said reproachfully, "is the editor of the *Northern Echo* and twenty-six other newspapers." (I was not really sure about my figures, but I felt it was no time to be mean with Sir Charles over a few newspapers).

"I have not heard of him," he said.

"Well," I said, "it's your turn now, anyway. Who do you know?"

We looked at each other through the dusty light of the room, and it seemed like a deadlock in the proceedings.

"Look here," he began, with a sudden flash of intelligence, "have you a passport?"

I had.

When he had it spread before him he read it aloud: "McClung, Nellie Letitia; married; eyes brown, mouth large."

He looked at me closely.

"By Jove! that's right," he cried. "Hair brown – slightly gray. That's right, too," apparently surprised at the coincidence.

Then he studied the photograph, comparing it with me.

"Don't you think it's a good picture?" I said.

He refused to commit himself. "It appears," he said at last, guardedly, "that you are the person described in this passport."

"Don't be rash," I said, "I would not like you to lose your job over this."

My sarcasm was lost.

"There is very little chance for fraud," he said, still regarding me critically.

"Fraud!" I cried hotly. "Fraud! You make me tired. Do you know, I can borrow money in any bank in Canada with less bother than this!"

"Quite!" he agreed with me. "Quite! I have always heard that the banking in Canada is done in very loose fashion. Very well, then," he said, "we will take your money."

Then it was my turn.

"Oh, indeed!" I said, "but remember I have my family traditions, too. You must convince me that you are to be trusted. Who are you? and what did your grandmother die of? I cannot leave my money with unauthorized people."

"Quite!" he said again, and solemnly placed before me the financial statement of the bank.

"And now," he said, "I will have to have a specimen signature for reference."

"Would you like a lock of my hair?" I asked.

"It will not be necessary," he replied gravely.

"And now, how shall we open this account?" I asked gaily. "Having gone so far I certainly want to see it done right. Just do whatever your custom is. Do we open with the National Anthem? Or, under the circumstances, would it not be better to use 'O Canada'?"

His air of perplexity deepened.

All went well until the day came when I returned to draw out my balance. Again I had to wait to see the manager.

"Look here," he began, "do I understand you are going away?"

"I am going on Friday," I said, "and I came in to draw my balance."

"This is Monday," he said, shutting one eye and transfixing me sternly with the other.

"Am I wrong again?" I asked. "Is Monday the wrong day to draw money?"

He pursed his mouth reflectively and beat his chin with his forefinger. "You should have given us more notice," he said at last.

I gasped. "Notice to draw fifty pounds?" I said. "Will you miss my account as much as that?"

"Certainly not," he corrected me, "but how are we to tell how many cheques you have issued?"

"You do not need to tell," I said; "I can talk, and I will tell you. The stubs in the cheque book will tell you."

"You may have written more than these," he persisted.

"But I didn't," I said.

"And it would be very embarrassing to have them presented after you had taken your money," he continued without heeding my interruption.

"It would be embarrassing for the holder of the cheque," I said, "but not for you."

"It would certainly embarrass us," he said virtuously, and here he looked at me with grave reproof; "and I should think it would embarrass you."

"Well, it won't," I said, "because I haven't written any but these."

He still hesitated.

"Well," I said, "do you think I had better cancel my sailing and stay another month to see if any other cheques come in?"

"Oh no, I do not advise that," he said.

"Well, then," I said, "get along in there and tell me my balance, and I'll write a cheque to cover it. I know what it is, but I just want to know if you do. Now chase yourself, my lad, for, pleasant as it is, I cannot stay all day talking to you."

He seemed to loom taller and grayer than ever, and the look he gave me was one of the deepest wonder.

But I got the money.

When our business relations were at an end he grew almost genial. "You will come again, I hope," he said; "and if you do I hope you will again open up an account with us."

"Oh, yes," I agreed, "surely I will. I couldn't think of going anywhere else. I would not care to break in another bank manager at my time of life. I will surely come to you – but do be careful," I said.

I know he will not be there when I go back. All depositors are not as long-suffering as I am. Someone will shoot him.

HOW IT FEELS TO BE A DEFEATED CANDIDATE

BY NELLIE L. MCCLUNG

From the angle of human interest defeat is more attractive than victory in as much as it is a more common experience, and the average reader may be described as a mind imbued with considerable fortitude, when contemplating the sorrows and disappointments of someone else.

Successful candidates are not given much scope in their speeches. They run in a pretty even groove. Borne down the street by the cheering throng which halted before the *Herald* building, with cries of "Speech! speech!" the successful candidate, carried aloft on the shoulders of his friends, addressed the surging sea of faces: "This is the proudest moment of my life... a man would be a dull clod who did not thrill... It will be my daily task to represent... this far-flung Dominion... your children's children... till death us do part!"

Not much to that!

But the story of how people receive the news of disaster admits of great variety. Do they rage, or weep? Do they bluff it off with a jest? Or do they call high heaven to witness? According to the latest picture version, the great man comes home early on election day, and there, in the seclusion of his own home, surrounded by a few trusted friends, calm, dignified, unmoved, mouth tight-lipped, head unbowed, face pale, but lighted by a valiant cheerfulness, he awaits the end!

And at a late hour, when all hope is dead, with the adverse majority steadily mounting like a meter of a taxi-cab wedged in the traffic, and wires of condolence beginning to arrive, carried thither by gray-uniformed boys in stiff caps, growing suddenly tired of it all, the great man bids his friends an affectionate good night, and goes heavily up the broad stairs, the light from the upper newel post falling full on his noble face, and showing the lines of care – and the friends below disperse quietly, murmuring something about one of whom the world was not worthy.

And so to bed!

We did not do it that way.

We all gathered in the committee rooms, which the night before had echoed with our laughter, our foolish boasts, and idle words, and before us on the wall a great blackboard bore the leering figures – that lurched and staggered before our eyes, changed every few minutes by one of the campaign managers. We were all frantically cheerful, but it was all about as merry as an empty bird-cage. With sickly smiles abounding, seen and unseen, we sang, "See him smiling," and "There's a Long, Long Trail," and speeches were made, and everyone did their best, but there is no denying the fact that there was an outcropping of gloom in the exercises of the evening. By ten o'clock we knew that one of our number was elected, one was defeated, and I was hovering between life and death. We knew that the counting would take all night, and some of the faithful ones were determined to see it through, but I was ready to call it a day about eleven o'clock, and leaving my political fate in the hands of the scrutineers, I came home, and slept until I heard the clip-clap of the milkman's horses, and the clinking of bottles on the back step, and through the open window I could see the crystal dawn leading in another day.

Then I remembered the unfinished business of the night before, but before consulting the telephone I looked out of the window for a while. It was so dewy green, and pleasant, and peaceful, with the shadows of the big trees making black lace medallions on the lawn.

The voice in the telephone was announcing the names of the elected candidates.

No! Mine was not among them. There were five elected. I stood sixth. Just for a moment I had a queer detached sensation, a bewildered, panicky feeling, and in that dizzy fragment of time, it came home to me that for all my philosophy and cheerful talk, I had never really believed I would be defeated – but now... now... the boat had actually sailed – without me.

But just like David in his grief, the mood quickly passed. Why should I go mourning all my days? My political hopes had died in the night! What of it? They were not the only hopes.

My family behaved admirably at breakfast, even the youngest one, who is at the age when it is rather embarrassing to have a mother of any sort, and particularly so to have one that goes out and gets herself defeated.

Thinking of the many women who would be disappointed, and men, too, was the heaviest part of my regret. I know how hard many of them had worked. I told myself over and over again that I did not mind... I suppose it does not require much fortitude to accept a stone wall... Anyway, I made a fine show of cheerfulness.

But though I went about quite light-heartedly and gay, telling myself and others how fine it felt to be free, and of how glad I was that I could go back to my own work with a clear conscience, there must have been some root of bitterness in me, for I was seized with a desire to cook, and I wanted the kitchen all to myself.

No woman can be utterly cast down who has a nice, bright, blue and white kitchen facing the west, with a good gas range, and blue and white checked linoleum on the floor (even if it is beginning to wear on the highways and market roads), a cook book, oilcloth covered and dropsical with loose-leaf additions, and the few odd trifles needed to carry out the suggestions.

I set off at once on a perfect debauch of cooking. I grated cheese, stoned dates, blanched almonds, whipped cream, set jelly – and let the phone ring.

It could tear itself out by the roots for all I cared. I was in another world – the pleasant, land-locked, stormless haven of double boilers, jelly molds, flour sifters, and other honest friends who make no promise they cannot carry through. The old stone sugar crock, with the cracked and handleless cup in it, seemed glad to see me, and even the gem jars, with their typed labels, sitting in a prim row, welcomed me back and asked no questions. I patted their little flat heads, and admitted that the years had been long; reminded them, too, that I had seen a lot more wear and tear than they had. I loved the feel of the little white-handled knife with which I peeled apples for pies. It lay comfortably in my hand and gave me the right vibration.

I am ashamed to have to tell it. But I got more comfort that day out of my cooking orgy than I did from either my philosophy or religion. But

I can see now, when the smoke of battle has cleared away, that I was the beneficiary of that great promise respecting the non-overflow of the rivers of sorrow. We often get blessings that we do not recognize at all, much less acknowledge. But God is not so insistent about having His gifts acknowledged as we are! So long as we get them!

No, there was no overflowing of sorrow. I think I could not have endured it if my biscuits had been heavy, or my date trifle tough, or the pie crust burnt in the bottom. Nothing failed me. And no woman can turn out an ovenful of flaky pies, crisply browned and spicily odorous, and not find peace for her troubled soul!

You've heard of the poet's heart leaping up when he beheld a rainbow in the sky! The same cardiac condition prevails when your salad dressing has that satiny texture, which is a cross between the skin of an egg and whipped cream!

The next day I wanted to get out. I craved free life, and fresh air, open fields and open sky. I wanted to look away to the mountains, blue in the distance, with the ice-caps on their heads. So I went to Earl Grey golf course, and played all morning. It was a morning of sparkling sunshine, and I loved all the little bluebells and violets that spangled the fairways. The mountains stood by mistily blue, with some snow in their crevices, cool and unconcerned.

The game was not entirely successful. I was too conscious of the Elbow Park houses below me; some of them vaguely resentful, some overbearingly exultant; and others leering at me with their drawn blinds, like half-closed conservative eyes. I tried to concentrate on the many good friends I have there, but some way the wires were crossed, the notes were jangled, and not a gleam of friendliness could I raise.

I got on better, and did some splendid driving by naming the balls, and was able by that means to give to one or two of them a pretty powerful poke.

I played each morning, and at the end of three days I saw that my spiritual health was restored – I was able then to dispassionately discuss the whole matter.

The confessional is psychologically sound, for whether it is a sin or a sorrow, or both, it is well to drag it out into the sunshine and let the healing winds blow over it. Ingrowing grief it is that festers and poisons.

So now I am able to bring down all the evidence. I believe, like Selina Peake's father, in "So Big," that every experience in life, pleasant or unpleasant, is so much velvet, if we know how to take it.

I believe that the way to take trouble is to leave it! I know there is in all of us, when things go wrong, a tendency to stick and stall, and explain, and amplify, and recall, and all that; and it is all worthless and unprofitable. There is no more devastating emotion than self-pity, it withers and sears the heart, dries up the fountain of youth, and is bad for the complexion! This is no coroner's inquest, no post-mortem on "How did it happen?"

I know how it happened that I was defeated. Not enough people wanted to have me elected! So there is no mystery about it – nothing that needs explanation.

But just why I thought I would be elected is a human interest story. I believe every candidate, who ran, believed in his own success. Hope springs eternal, and friends see to it that it does. Prior to election day, friends fairly bubble with enthusiasm. They haven't a doubt or a fear in the world! They tell you the enemy concedes your election! The bets are all on you! I remember, though I did not think of it until after the election, that when a certain man ran for mayor in Edmonton some years ago, he had more names on his nomination papers than votes on election day!

Then there were the departing friends who earnestly desired to do their country one good turn before they left for their holidays. They came to see me. The first one said: "My dear, you simply must let your name go before the convention. We need you in the House. And after your five years of experience! You simply must not think of dropping out! What chance? – Oh, my dear! Everyone says you will head the polls. The baker spoke to me about you this morning. It seems his wife was in your Bible class in Manitoba. He's so sorry he's an American citizen, and so neither of them can vote, but they'll work for you."

I was greatly touched by her enthusiasm. I thought she must be a type of many. So she was. I met them everywhere. They sought me out, and entreated me to step out and save my country, and then having nobly performed their duty as citizens, one by one they sought the solace of the cool, sweet far distant places, where birds voices call, and waters idly lap the shore.

But they didn't forget me! On election day, they sent me picture postcards, and in fairness I must add that at least three of them came back to vote for me.

Looking back on it now I see I went through the campaign with a sort of courageous imbecility! So many people told me I was sure to be elected, I seemed to forget that I had deep-seated, relentless antagonism from several sections of the community. Naturally, my opponents did not report to me, and I reasoned, apparently, from insufficient data. But, a few friends full of enthusiasm can create quite an impression. Mine appeared like an army with banners. I should have remembered that there was nothing remarkable, or significant, about this. Everyone has some friends. The blackboards in front of the filling stations carried a wise word the other day. They said:

"Even cotton stockings have their supporters!"

I might have known that the liquor interests do not forgive the people who oppose them. Temperance people will forget their friends and cheerfully forgive their enemies at election time, but the liquor people are more dependable. Some of them spoke to me about my stand on prohibition, and told me quite frankly that if I would put the soft pedal on the liquor question they would vote for me.

And I didn't. And they didn't. And there are no hard feelings between us.

One grand old exponent of the cup that cheers and inebriates told me, with odorous conviction, that he was with me against the hard stuff, but a glass of beer never hurt any one! And then he told me sweetly reminiscent tales of his dear old sainted grandfather and other godly and rotund gentlemen of the old school who drank heavily and regularly – and died in the hope of a glorious resurrection.

But far more bitter and unyielding was the opposition of the conservative element (my own party is not entirely free from it), that resents the invasion of women. Public offices, particularly those that carry emoluments, they believe to belong, by the ancient right of possession, to men. They are quite willing to let women work on boards, or committees, or indeed anywhere if the work is done gratuitously – but if there is a salary, they know at once that women are not fitted by nature for that! And God never intended them to be exposed to the dangers and temptations incident to such a post!

The dangers and temptations incident to office-cleaning at night, which is done by women, and the lonely homeward walk in the early morning when there are no cars running, is not so bad, for the work is sufficiently ill-paid to keep it quite womanly.

And the curious part of this is that women can be found who will support this view. Not many – and not thinking women, just a few who bitterly resent having any woman go farther than they are ever likely to go.

Another feature, which works against any woman who runs for public office, is the subconscious antagonism of men who don't want to work with women. Men are subconsciously afraid of women! Afraid they will not play fair! No individual man is to blame – it is a racial trait, and will take a lot of working out. Men will work their fingers to the bone for women – but not with them.

And then, of course, opposing me were many wives! No one should criticize the wives! And I won't! I saw many of them on election day. One told me quite sweetly – "I don't know anything about this, but Charley is frightfully keen, and told me to give out these cards, and say 'I hope you will vote our ticket' – It's all a beastly muddle to me – and bores me to tears!"

I thought of Mrs. Pankhurst and her heroic followers going to jail, and suffering the agonies of social ostracism, as well as physical cruelty, to win for women like these the right to vote, and with a less worthy emotion I thought of some of the efforts we had made here. I was like the young chap of five who denounced his one-year-old sister when she displeased him, in these scathing words: "I am sorry I ever prayed for you!"

Oh, well!

Life has compensation for all of us. When one door shuts – another opens.

Basil King told us once, that the day he met with the accident that made it impossible to carry on his work as a clergyman, he bought a typewriter. I didn't need to buy one. All mine needed was a new ribbon.

NOTES

CHAPTER 1

[1]Nellie L. McClung, *Clearing in the West* (Toronto: Thomas Allen & Son, Ltd., 1935), pp. 146–150.

[2]"Mrs. Nellie L. McClung: A Prophet Who Is Not without Honor in Her Own Country," *Manitoba Free Press*, undated clipping, McClung Papers. BC Archives & Records Service, Victoria, BC, Nellie McClung Collection, Add. Mss. 10.

[3]Nellie L. McClung, *The Stream Runs Fast* (Toronto: Thomas Allen & Son, Ltd., 1945), p. 77.

[4]McClung, *Clearing in the West,* p. 36.

[5]Ibid., p. 35.

[6]McClung, *The Stream Runs Fast,* p. 59.

[7]Ibid., p. 174.

[8]McClung, "It Was Loaded," in *Flowers for the Living* (Toronto: Thomas Allen & Son, Ltd., 1931), p. 46.

[9]"Mrs. Nellie McClung at Rea's," column in *The Canadian White Ribbon Tidings* (November 1, 1915), p. 255.

[10]Nellie L. McClung, "The Writer's Creed," typescript of a speech, McClung Papers.

[11]McClung, *Clearing in the West,* p. 339.

[12]Promotional review of *Clearing in the West,* undated clipping, McClung Papers.

[13]McClung, "The Writer's Creed."

[14]Nellie L. McClung, untitled, undated typescript, McClung Papers.

[15]Nellie L. McClung, "The Social Responsibilities of Women," typescript of a speech, McClung Papers.

[16]Ibid.

[17]Nellie L. McClung, *In Times Like These* (Toronto: McLeod and Allen, 1915), pp. 126–7.

[18]Candace Savage, *Our Nell* (Saskatoon: Western Producer Prairie Books, 1979), pp. 104–5.

[19]McClung, *Clearing in the West,* pp. 281–2.

[20]McClung, *The Stream Runs Fast,* p. 61.

[21]Ibid., p. 235.

[22]McClung, Mark. "Portrait of My Mother." Typescript of speech he made at Nellie McClung Conference, University of Guelph, September 26–28, 1975. This is available from Dr. Margaret Andersen, Department of Languages, University of Guelph, Guelph, Ontario.

[23]"The First Great Prohibition Parade Ever Held in Canada," *The Canadian White Ribbon Tidings* (January 1916), pp. 5–6. No author named.

[24]McClung, *The Stream Runs Fast,* p. 211.

[25]Savage, p. 145.

[26]Ibid., p. 52.

CHAPTER 2

[1]"Address to Ministerial Association of Methodist Church," undated typescript, McClung Papers.

[2]Pauline Ashton, "Windy Nellie: The Canadian Woman's Best Friend," *Weekend Magazine* (December 15, 1973), pp. 18–19.

[3]McClung, *The Stream Runs Fast,* p. 145.

[4]Ibid.

[5]Ibid., pp. 146–8.

[6]Patricia Louise Verkruysse, "Small Legacy of Truth: The Novels of Nellie McClung." M.A. Thesis, University of New Brunswick, 1973.

[7]McClung, *The Second Chance,* pp. 127–8.

[8]Nellie L. McClung, untitled typescript, McClung Papers.

[9]Nellie L. McClung, "I'll Never Tell My Age Again," *Maclean's Magazine* (March 15, 1926), p. 56.

[10]Savage, *Our Nell,* p. 202.

[11]Nellie L. McClung, "Well-Wishers," *The Life Underwriters News* (August 24, 1919), p. 47.

[12]Savage, *Our Nell,* quote taken from the *Carman Standard* (June 11, 1914).

[13]"Politics Are an Uncut Book for Women, Nellie McClung Declares," undated clipping from *The Calgary News-Telegraph,* McClung Papers.

[14]"Mrs. Nellie McClung's Challenge to the People of the East," *The Citizen* (Friday, October 22, 1915), clipping, McClung Papers.

[15]McClung, *The Stream Runs Fast,* pp. 106–7.

[16]Ibid., p. 115.

[17]"How the Vote Was Not Won – Burlesqued in Women's Parliament," *Winnipeg Tribune* (January 29, 1914), clipping, McClung Papers.

[18]Alison Craig, "Over the Tea-Cups," 1914, newspaper clipping, McClung Papers.

[19]"They Expect of Women What They Don't of Men," undated clipping, source not identified, McClung Papers.

CHAPTER 3

[1]McClung, *In Times Like These,* pp. 112–3.

[2]Ibid., p. 108.

[3]Modern feminists have also felt that it is important to break imposed silences. See Mary Daly, "Theology after the Demise of God the Father: A Call for the Castration of Sexist Religion" in *Sexist Religion and Women in the Church,* ed., Alice L. Hageman (New York: Association Press, 1974), p. 130. Beverly Wildung Harrison, "Sexism and the Contemporary Church: When Evasion becomes Complicity," in Hageman, pp. 204–5.

[4]Hageman, p. 109.

[5]McClung, *In Times Like These,* p. 115.

[6]Ibid., p. 103.

[7]"Mrs. Nellie McClung's Challenge to the People of the East," op. cit.

[8]*Proceedings of the Fifth Ecumenical Methodist Conference* (Toronto: The Methodist Book and Publishing House, 1921), pp. 257–8.

[9]Ibid., p. 259.

[10]Mary E. Hallett, "Nellie McClung and the Fight for the Ordination of Women in the United Church of Canada," *Atlantis* (Spring, 1979) 4, p. 8.

[11]The account of this correspondence is in a typescript article, "The Woman Who Can Hold Her Tongue," undated, McClung Papers.

[12]This was part of a survey initiated by Lynne (Hannon) Bandy, Peter Short and Carol Hancock for a course at Emmanuel College, Toronto, 1975.

[13]Nellie L. McClung, Letter to the Editor, *The New Outlook* (December 19, 1928), pp. 14, 26.

[14]Hallett, p. 10

[15]"Ordination of Women to Ministry Left Undecided," clipping, McClung Papers. The date, judging from the content of the article, was probably Friday, September 14, 1928. Of the title of the newspaper, all that is visible is *Free Press Eve...*

[16]McClung, "A Retrospect," p. 1.

[17]Incomplete notes, both typescript and handwritten, McClung Papers.

[18]Ruth Compton Brouwer, "The Canadian Methodist Church and Ecclesiastical Suffrage for Women 1902–1914," unpublished paper, United Church Archives, p. 12.

[19]Lotta Dempsey, "Mrs. McClung Successfully Champions Ordination of Fair Sex Before Large Audience," January 31, 1929, unidentified newspaper clipping, McClung Papers.

[20]Nellie L. McClung, *More Leaves from Lantern Lane* (Toronto: Thomas Allen & Son, Ltd., 1937), pp. 184–6.

[21]Louise H. Mahood, *The History of Ordained Women Ministers in the United Church of Canada.* Honors Thesis for Bachelor of Arts, History and Women's Studies, university unidentified, April 16, 1984.

CHAPTER 4

[1]Nellie L. McClung, *Be Good to Yourself* (Toronto: Thomas Allen & Son, Ltd., 1930), p. 164.

[2]Ibid., pp. 156–160.

[3]Nellie L. McClung, "Success," *White Ribbon Bulletin* (December 1916), p. 180. Clipping, McClung Papers.

[4]Carol Lee Bacchi, *Liberation Deferred? The Ideas of the English-Canadian Suffragists, 1877–1918* (Toronto: The University of Toronto Press, 1983), pp. 32–33.

[5]McClung, *Be Good to Yourself,* pp. 146-51.

[6]Harrison, in Hageman, pp. 199–200. The definition, brought forward by Harrison, is credited to Elizabeth Janeway.

[7]McClung, *In Times Like These,* p. 108.

[8]Gwen Matheson and V.E. Lang, "Nellie McClung: Not A Nice Lady," in *Women in the Canadian Mosaic,* ed. Gwen Matheson (Toronto: Peter Martin Associates Limited, 1976), p. 16.

[9]Linda Kealey, ed., *A Not Unreasonable Claim: Women and Reform in Canada, 1880s–1920s* (Toronto: The Women's Press, 1979), p. 7.

[10]This opinion is held by both Carol Bacchi and Beverley Harrison.

[11]Kealey, p. 9.

[12]Wayne Roberts, "Rocking the Cradle for the World: The New Woman and Maternal Feminism, Toronto, 1877–1914," in Kealey, p. 19.

[13]Mariana Valverde, "The Nurturant Suffragists," *Broadside* 4 (July 1983): 9–10.

[14]McClung, *In Times Like These,* p. 73.

[15]McClung, "A Retrospect," p. 3.

Chapter 5

[1]Nellie L. McClung, "What Religion Means to Me," *The Quest* V (March 29, 1942): p. 197.

[2]The excerpt comes from a script of the broadcast made by McClung on November 16, 1939, for the National Night of the Business and Professional Women's Club, McClung Papers.

[3]McClung, "What Religion Means to Me," p. 196.

[4]Nellie L. McClung, *The Next of Kin,* (Toronto: Thomas Allen & Son, Ltd., 1917), p. 219.

[5]Ibid.

[6]Ibid., p. 218.

[7]Nellie L. McClung, "Well-Wishers," p. 49.

[8]"Mrs. Nellie L. McClung: A Prophet Who Is Not without Honor in Her Own Country," undated clipping from an unidentified Manitoba newspaper, circa 1915.

[9]McClung, *In Times Like These,* p. 21.

[10]Nellie L. McClung, *Sowing Seeds in Danny* (Toronto: William Briggs, 1911), pp. 270–1.

[11]Nellie L. McClung, *The Second Chance* (Toronto: William Briggs, 1912), p. 211.

[12]McClung, *The Stream Runs Fast,* p. 69.

[13]McClung, *The Next of Kin,* p. 211.

[14]McClung, *In Times Like These,* p. 32.

[15]Nellie L. McClung, "Has Religion a Place in Wartime?" newspaper clipping, handwritten date, August 3, 1940, McClung Papers.

[16]Undated clipping from the *Free Press News Bulletin,* Winnipeg, McClung Papers.

[17]Nellie L. McClung, "Are We Disturbed?" *Evening Citizen* (May 15, 1937), clipping in McClung Papers.

[18]Nellie L. McClung, "What's the Matter with the Church?" *Victoria Daily Times* (Saturday, January 18, 1941), p. 2, magazine section.

[19]"The Religion of Labor," undated typescript in McClung Papers.

[20]McClung, *The Next of Kin,* p. 229.

[21]Nellie L. McClung, *Leaves from Lantern Lane* (Toronto: Thomas Allen & Son, Ltd., 1936), p. 135.

[22]McClung, *In Times Like These,* p. 119.

[23]McClung, "A Retrospect," p. 3.

[24]Ibid., p. 105.

[25]Letty Russell, in Hageman, p. 48.

[26]Richard Allen, "The Background of the Social Gospel in Canada," in *The Social Gospel in Canada,* ed. Richard Allen (Ottawa: National Museums of Canada, 1975), pp. 4–5.

[27]Benjamin G. Smillie, "The Social Gospel in Canada: A Theological Critique," in *The Social Gospel in Canada,* ed. Richard Allen (Ottawa: National Museums of Canada, 1975), p. 322.

Chapter 6

[1]McClung, *In Times Like These,* pp. 8–9.

[2]The story is told by McClung in *Clearing in the West,* pp. 167–80.

[3]Ibid., pp. 304–9.

[4]McClung, "A Retrospect," *The Country Guide* (December 2, 1929), p. 3.

[5]Ibid.

[6]McClung, *In Times Like These*, p. 6.

[7]David B. Guralnik, Editor in Chief, *Webster's New World Dictionary* (Toronto: Nelson, Foster & Scott Ltd., 1970), p. 26.

[8]Nellie L. McClung, "How Prohibition Has Worked in Canada," typescript article, undated, volume 24, McClung Papers.

[9]McClung, *In Times Like These*, p. 6.

[10]McClung, "Can a Woman Raise a Family and Have a Career?" *Maclean's* (February 15, 1928), p. 70.

[11]Ibid., p. 71

[12]McClung, *In Times Like These*, pp. 44–5.

[13]Ibid., p. 94.

[14]Ibid., p. 58.

[15]This particular quote comes from a newspaper clipping entitled "Mrs. Nellie McClung Campaigns in Minneapolis"; this same material, however is included in the chapter "Hardy perennials!" in *In Times Like These*. This material appears in many locations since it formed the bulk of her speech and article content around the years in which the book was published. In this instance the newspaper was covering a speech made by McClung to the Mississippi Valley Suffrage Association. (Clipping, from the McClung file in the Glenbow Institute, handwritten date, 9/5/16)

[16]Untitled book review of *In Times Like These*, carried Wed., Nov. 10, 1915, in Edmonton paper, but which originated with Toronto Globe. Clipping, McClung Papers.

[17]McClung, *In Times Like These*, pp. 57–8.

[18]Ibid., pp. 58–9.

[19]McClung, "The Social Responsibilities of Women."

[20]Ruth Compton Brouwer, "The Canadian Methodist Church and Ecclesiastical Suffrage for Women 1902–1914," unpublished paper, United Church Archives, p. 3.

[21]McClung, "A Retrospect," p. 58.

[22]Nellie L. McClung, *More Leaves from Lantern Lane* (Toronto: Thomas Allen & Son, Ltd., 1937), p. 162.

[23]"Mrs. Nellie McClung Campaigns in Minneapolis."

[24]McClung, *The Stream Runs Fast*, pp. 181–2.

[25]Nellie L. McClung, speech to the U.F.A. Convention, undated typescript, McClung Papers.

[26]McClung, "The Social Responsibilities of Women."

[27]Ibid.

[28]"Mrs. Nellie McClung Campaigns in Minneapolis."

[29]McClung, *The Stream Runs Fast*, p. 172.

[30]McClung, "The Last Reserves," *The Next of Kin*, pp. 227–240. This is just one of the articles carrying that theme.

CHAPTER 7

[1]McClung, "A Retrospect," p. 3.

[2]Byrne Hope Sanders, *Emily Murphy: Crusader* (Toronto: The Macmillan Company of Canada Limited, 1945), p. 141. This is a useful source of material on this whole case.

[3]Norman Lambert, "A Joan of the West," *Canadian Magazine,* January, 1916.

[4]Eleanor Harman, "Five Persons from Alberta," in *The Clear Spirit,* ed. Mary Quayle Innis (Toronto: University of Toronto Press, 1966), p. 171.

[5]Candace Savage, *Foremothers* (Regina: Pamphlet produced with the support of the Saskatchewan Government), p. 38.

[6]Linda Rasmussen, Lorna Rasmussen, Candace Savage and Anne Wheeler, *A Harvest Yet to Reap,* (Toronto: The Women's Press, 1976), p. 204.

[7]Harman, p. 172.

[8]Catherine Cleverdon, *The Woman Suffrage Movement in Canada* (Toronto: University of Toronto Press, 1950; reprint ed., Toronto: University of Toronto Press, 1975), p. 149.

[9]Sanders, p. 238.

[10]Letter from Emily Murphy to Nellie L. McClung, January 10, 1927, McClung Papers.

[11]McClung, *The Stream Runs Fast,* pp. 188–9.

[12]Emily Murphy, letter addressed to "My Dear Nellie L." from "Old J.C." [Janey Canuck, Murphy's pen name], dated March 4, 1930, McClung Papers.

[13]Anne Squire, "In 50 Years, How Much Progress for Women as 'Persons'?" *The United Church Observer,* 43 (October 1979) p. 11.

[14]Ramsay Cook and Wendy Mitchinson, editors, *The Proper Sphere* (Toronto: Oxford University Press, Canadian Branch, 1976), p. 289.

[15]Ibid., pp. 290–1.

[16]McClung, *The Stream Runs Fast,* p. x.

CHAPTER 8

[1]McClung, *The Stream Runs Fast,* pp. 127–130.

[2]Wm. Arthur Deacon, "A Western Woman," *Mail and Empire* (Toronto: Saturday, November 9, 1935), clipping, McClung Papers.

[3]Natalie Symmes, "Nellie McClung of the West: Writer, Lecturer, Cake Baker, Politician, Methodist, Mother." *The Canadian White Ribbon Tidings* (July 1916).

[4]A clipping of a column entitled "Personal Stuff," by "E.E.R.," McClung Papers. A note in McClung's handwriting deciphers that as Elmer E. Roper and adds: "Edmonton, November 1938."

[5]Emily Murphy, "What Janey Thinks of Nellie," *Maclean's Magazine* (September 1, 1921), pp. 15, 34–35.

[6]Savage, *Our Nell,* p. 1 of the Preface.

[7]Interview of Savage by C.L. Hancock in 1981.

[8]Veronica Strong-Boag, introduction to reprinted edition of Nellie L. McClung's *In Times Like These* (Toronto: University of Toronto Press, 1972), p. xix.

[9]Ibid., p. viii.

[10]Gwen Matheson, "Nellie McClung," *Canadian Dimension,* (June 1975) 10, p. 46.

[11]Strong-Boag, p. xx.

[12]Veronica Strong-Boag, "Canadian Feminism in the 1920s: The Case of Nellie L. McClung," *Journal of Canadian Studies* (Summer 1977) 12, p. 65.

[13]Patricia Connelly's *Last Hired, First Fired* (Toronto: Women's Press, 1978) provides a very helpful analysis of the inter-relatedness of women in the Canadian work force and the Canadian economy.

[14]Strong-Boag, "Feminism," p. 66.

[15]Mary Daly mentions the incident in *Beyond God The Father* (Boston: Beacon Press, 1973) pp. 144–145, but her article "The Women's Movement: An Exodus Community," *Religious Education* (September 1972) contains the sermon and reflections upon the event by some women who participated.

CHAPTER 9

[1]McClung, *The Stream Runs Fast,* p. xiii.

[2]Verkruysse, p. 204.

[3]Ibid., p. 56.

[4]Strong-Boag, introduction to *In Times Like These,* p. xix.

[5]Gwen Matheson and V.E. Lang, *Women in the Canadian Mosaic* (Toronto: Peter Martin Associates, 1976) p. 19. One can contrast Strong-Boag's categorization with Matheson and Lang's assessment: "... if Nellie's Irish background made her seek out laughter, her Scottish derivation made her tenacious. These qualities along with the influence of her environment resulted in a *particularly Canadian brand of feminism* – acknowledging the complexity of human problems rather than reducing everything to a single issue, not tolerating fools gladly and yet being, on the whole, good-humored rather than rancorous, preferring the bite of wit to the vehemence of denunciation." (Emphasis mine.)

[6]Nellie L. McClung, "Speak Up! Ladies!" *Canadian Home Journal* (November 1919).

[7]Nellie L. McClung, "Defensive Common-Sense," typescript, McClung Papers.

[8]McClung, *The Stream Runs Fast,* p. 143.

[9]Savage, pp. 137–8.

[10]Mary Daly, "Theology after the Demise of God the Father: A Call for the Castration of Sexist Religion," in *Sexist Religion and Women in the Church* ed. Alice L. Hageman (New York: Association Press, 1974), p. 140.

[11]Henry H. Mitchell, *The Recovery of Preaching* San Francisco: Harper and Row, 1977), pp. 1, 3–4, 7.

[12]Mark McClung, "Portrait of My Mother."

[13]Reinhold Niebuhr, "Humour and Faith," in *Discerning the Signs of the Times* (London: S.C.M. Press, 1946).

[14]McClung, *The Stream Runs Fast,* p. 110.

[15]Ibid., p. 134.

[16]McClung, "The Last Reserves," pp. 239–240.

BIBLIOGRAPHY

PRIMARY SOURCES

BOOKS BY NELLIE L. MCCLUNG

All We Like Sheep. Toronto: Thomas Allen & Son, Ltd., 1931.

Be Good to Yourself. Toronto: Thomas Allen & Son, Ltd., 1930.

The Black Creek Stopping House. Toronto: William Briggs, 1912.

Clearing in the West: My Own Story. Toronto: Thomas Allen & Son, Ltd., 1935.

Flowers for the Living. Toronto: Thomas Allen & Son, Ltd., 1931.

In Times Like These. Toronto: McLeod and Allen, 1915; reprinted Toronto: University of Toronto Press, 1975.

Leaves from Lantern Lane. Toronto: Thomas Allen & Son, Ltd., 1936.

More Leaves from Lantern Lane. Toronto: Thomas Allen & Son, Ltd., 1937.

The Next of Kin. Toronto: Thomas Allen & Son, Ltd., 1917.

Painted Fires. Toronto: Thomas Allen & Son, Ltd., 1925.

Purple Springs. Toronto: Thomas Allen & Son, Ltd., 1921.

The Second Chance. Toronto: William Briggs, 1910.

Sowing Seeds in Danny. Toronto: William Briggs, 1908.

The Stream Runs Fast: My Own Story. Toronto: Thomas Allen & Son, Ltd., 1945.

Three Times and Out: A Canadian Boy's Experience in Germany. Boston: Houghton Mifflin, 1918.

When Christmas Crossed "The Peace." 1923.

ARTICLES BY NELLIE L. MCCLUNG

"A Retrospect." *The Country Guide,* December 2, 1929. pp. 3, 58.

"Are We Disturbed?" *Evening Citizen,* May 15, 1937. Clipping, McClung Papers. BC Archives & Records Service, Victoria, BC, Nellie McClung Collection, Add. Mss. 10.

"Banking in London." In *All We Like Sheep,* Toronto: Thomas Allen & Son, Ltd., 1926.

"Before They Call." Pamphlet. Toronto: Board of Home Missions, The United Church of Canada, 1937.

"Can a Woman Raise a Family and Have a Career?" *Maclean's Magazine,* February 1928. pp. 10, 70–1, 75.

"Has Religion a Place in Wartime?" Clipping, McClung Papers.

"How It Feels to Be a Defeated Candidate." In *Be Good to Yourself,* Toronto: Thomas Allen & Son, Ltd., 1930.

"How Prohibition Has Worked in Canada," Typescript, McClung Papers.

"Religion of Labour." Undated typescript, McClung Papers.

"Shall Women Preach?" *Chatelaine*, September 1934. pp. 14–15.

"The Social Responsibilities of Women." Typescript of a speech, McClung Papers.

"Speak Up! Ladies!" *Canadian Home Journal*, November 1919.

"Speaking of Women." *Maclean's Magazine*, May 1916. pp. 25–6, 96–7.

"Thrift." *Canadian Home Journal*, September 1916. Clipping, McClung Papers.

"Well-Wishers." *The Life Underwriters News*, August 24, 1919. pp. 47–9.

"What Religion Means to Me." *The Quest*, V (March 29, 1942) pp. 193–4, 197, 206.

"What's the Matter with the Church?" *Victoria Daily Times*, Saturday, January 18, 1941. p. 2. Magazine Section.

"The Writer's Creed." Typescript, McClung Papers.

Secondary Sources

Books

Allen, Richard. "The Background of the Social Gospel in Canada." In *The Social Gospel in Canada*. Edited by Richard Allen. Ottawa: National Museums of Canada, 1975.

— ed. *The Social Gospel of Canada*. Ottawa: National Museums of Canada, 1975.

— *The Social Passion*. Toronto: The University of Toronto Press, 1973.

Bacchi, Carol Lee. *Liberation Deferred? The Ideas of the English-Canadian Suffragists, 1877–1918*. Toronto: The University of Toronto Press, 1983.

Connelly, Patricia. *Last Hired, First Fired: Women and the Canadian Work Force*. Toronto: The Women's Press, 1978.

Daly, Mary. *Beyond God the Father*. Boston: Beacon Press, 1973.

— "Theology after the Demise of God the Father: A Call for the Castration of Sexist Religion." In *Sexist Religion and Women in the Church*. Edited by Alice L. Hageman. New York: Association Press, 1974.

Guralnik, David B., editor in chief. *Webster's New World Dictionary*. Toronto: Nelson, Foster and Scott Ltd., 1970.

Hageman, Alice L., ed. *Sexist Religion and Women in the Church*. New York: Association Press, 1974.

— "Introduction: No More Silence!" In *Sexist Religion and Women in the Church*, New York: Association Press, 1974.

Harrison, Beverly Wildung. "Sexism and the Contemporary Church: When Evasion Becomes Complicity." In *Sexist Religion and Women in the Church*. Edited by Alice L. Hageman. New York: Association Press, 1974.

Kealey, ed. *A Not Unreasonable Claim: Women and Reform in Canada, 1880s–1920s*. Toronto: The Women's Press, 1979.

Matheson, Gwen, ed. *Women in the Canadian Mosaic*. Toronto: Peter Martin Associates, 1976.

Matheson Gwen, and Lang, V.E. "Nellie McClung: Not a Nice Lady," *Women in the Canadian Mosaic*. Toronto: The Women's Press, 1979. pp. 1–20.

Mitchell, Henry H. *The Recovery of Preaching*. San Francisco: Harper and Row, 1977.

Niebuhr, Reinhold. *Discerning the Signs of the Times*. London: S.C.M. Press, 1946.

Proceedings of the Fifth Ecumenical Methodist Conference. Toronto: The Methodist Book and Publishing House, 1921.

Roberts, Wayne. "'Rocking the Cradle for the World': The New Woman and Maternal Feminism, Toronto, 1877–1914." In *A Not Unreasonable Claim: Women and Reform in Canada, 1880s–1920s.* Edited by Linda Kealey. Toronto: The Women's Press, 1979.

Sanders, Byrne Hope. *Emily Murphy: Crusader.* Toronto: The Macmillan Company, 1945.

Savage, Candace. *Our Nell.* Saskatoon: Western Producer Prairie Books, 1979.

Smillie, Benjamin G. "The Social Gospel in Canada: A Theological Critique." In *The Social Gospel in Canada.* Edited by Richard Allen. Ottawa: National Museums of Canada, 1975.

ARTICLES

Ashton, Pauline. "Windy Nellie, The Canadian Woman's Best Friend," *Weekend Magazine.* December 15, 1973. pp. 18–19.

Daly, Mary. "The Women's Movement: An Exodus Community," *Religious Education.* September 1972.

Deacon, Wm. Arthur. "A Western Woman," *Mail and Empire.* Saturday, November 9, 1935. Clipping, McClung Papers.

"The First Great Prohibition Parade Ever Held in Canada," *The Canadian White Ribbon Tidings.* January, 1916. pp. 5-6.

Gorham, Deborah. "Singing up the Hill," *Canadian Dimension.* 10. (June, 1975) pp. 26–38.

Hallett, Mary E. "Nellie McClung and the Fight for the Ordination of Women in the United Church of Canada." *Atlantis.* Spring, 1979. pp. 2–16.

Lambert, Norman. "A Joan of the West," *Canadian Magazine,* January 1916, pp. 265–9.

Matheson, Gwen. "Nellie McClung," *Canadian Dimension.* 10. (June 1975) pp. 42–48.

"Mrs. Nellie McClung at Rea's." *The Canadian White Ribbon Tidings.* November 1, 1915. p. 255.

"Mrs. Nellie McClung's Challenge to the People of the East," *The Citizen.* Friday, October 22, 1915. Clipping, McClung Papers.

Murphy, Emily. "What Janey Thinks of Nellie," *Maclean's Magazine.* September 1, 1921. pp. 14, 34–5.

"Nellie McClung Says Task of Women is to Mend War-Torn World." November 2, 1917. Clipping, United Church Archives.

"Ordination of Women to Ministry Left Undecided." Clipping, McClung Papers.

Raper, Elmer E. "Personal Stuff." Clipping, McClung Papers.

Strong-Boag, Veronica. "Introduction," *In Times Like These.* Toronto: University of Toronto Press, 1972.

— "Canadian Feminism in the 1920s: The Case of Nellie L. McClung." *Journal of Canadian Studies.* 12. (Summer, 1977) pp. 58–68.

Symmes, Natalie. "Nellie McClung of the West: Writer, Lecturer, Cake Baker, Politician, Methodist, Mother," *The Canadian White Ribbon Tidings.* July 1916. pp. 217–19, 232.

Valverde, Mariana. "The Nurturant Suffragists." *Broadside* 4 (July 1983) pp. 9–10.

Zieman, Margaret K. "Nellie Was a Lady Terror." *Maclean's Magazine,* October 1, 1953, pp. 21, 62–66.

Theses

Brouwer, Ruth Compton. "The Canadian Methodist Church and Ecclesiastical Suffrage for Women 1902–1914." Unpublished thesis. United Church Archives.

Clifton, Lloyd M. "Nellie McClung: A Representative of the Canadian Social Gospel Movement." Master of Theology Thesis. Knox College, Toronto, 1979.

Mahood, Louise H. "The History of Ordained Women Ministers in the United Church of Canada." Honors Thesis for Bachelor of Arts. 1984.

Verkruysse, Patricia Louise. "Small Legacy of Truth: The Novels of Nellie McClung." M.A. Thesis. University of New Brunswick, 1973.

INDEX